Alexander George Richey

The Irish land Laws

Alexander George Richey

The Irish land Laws

ISBN/EAN: 9783743330467

Manufactured in Europe, USA, Canada, Australia, Japa

Cover: Foto ©ninafisch / pixelio.de

Manufactured and distributed by brebook publishing software (www.brebook.com)

Alexander George Richey

The Irish land Laws

THE
IRISH LAND LAWS

BY

ALEXANDER G. RICHEY, Q.C., LL.D.

DEPUTY REGIUS PROFESSOR OF FEUDAL AND ENGLISH LAW
IN THE UNIVERSITY OF DUBLIN

London
MACMILLAN AND CO.
1880

All rights reserved

'Et requit à Gargantua, qu'il instituast sa religion au contraire de toutes autres.'

PREFACE.

The object of this work is not to discuss the Irish Land Question from either an economic or political point of view, nor to propose any specific alteration in the existing law, nor indeed to suggest that any such alteration should be made.

It aims at no more than to afford to those who desire to study the subject practically, in an untechnical and popular form, some, perhaps useful, information upon the following points: the legal theory of the hiring of land; the rules relative thereto elaborated by the civil lawyers and adopted by the French Code; the rules of the English Law upon the subject; and the alterations in the latter introduced into the Irish Law by the Acts of the 23 and 24 Vict. ch. 154, and 33 and 34 Vict. ch. 46;

and also to suggest certain questions which must be seriously considered by those who would frame a new Landlord and Tenant Code for Ireland, or further amend the existing system.

The extracts from Pothier are all taken from the short treatise 'Du Contrat de Bail à Rente,' and those from the Code Napoléon from the 8th title of the Third Book 'Du Contrat de Louage,' and specific references have not therefore been appended to the text.

The Acts of the 23 & 24 Vict. c. 145 and 33 & 34 Vict. c. 46, and the judicial decisions thereupon, are published in an available form in 'The Statutes relating to the Law of Landlord and Tenant in Ireland since 1860,' by F. Nolan and R. R. Kane, Third Edition.

A. G. R.

CONTENTS.

CHAPTER		PAGE
	INTRODUCTION	1
I.	CUSTOMARY TENURES	4
II.	CONVENTIONAL TENURES	7
III.	THE CODE NAPOLÉON	21
IV.	THE FRENCH LAW AS TO 'AMÉLIORATION'	26
V.	LEADING PRINCIPLES OF THE FRENCH LAW	32
VI.	THE ENGLISH LANDLORD AND TENANT LAW AS SUBSISTING IN IRELAND PRIOR TO 1860	34
VII.	THE LANDLORD AND TENANT ACT, 1860	47
VIII.	THE RESULTS OF THE ACT OF 1860	57
IX.	THE IRISH LAND ACT OF 1870	62
	LEADING PROVISIONS OF THIS ACT	66
	THE BRIGHT CLAUSES	81
	TENANT RIGHT	100
	QUESTIONS FOR CONSIDERATION	108

APPENDIX.

POPULAR ERRORS AS TO IRISH LAW . . 115

THE IRISH LAND LAWS.

INTRODUCTION.

DURING the past year many articles have been written, and speeches made, advocating alterations, more or less extensive, in the Irish Law of Landlord and Tenant, and suggesting new legislation whereby the relations of the owners and occupiers of land in Ireland may be established upon a permanent and satisfactory basis.

When the abolition or reform of any system of law is taken in hand, it is of the first importance that the enactments of the existing code should be clearly understood; nothing is more dangerous than a partial repeal of legal principles, which leaves other rules, which are either their logical antecedents or consequences, still subsisting; or an ill-considered reform which leaves mingled together in hopeless confusion enactments of different origin and contradictory nature.

It must be confessed that many of those who have dealt lately with this subject have failed to master the changes produced in the Irish Law of Landlord and Tenant by the Acts of 1860 and 1870, and have proceeded upon the assumption that the law as it now exists is the same as that which subsisted prior to the former date. It is not to be expected that laymen should take upon themselves the irksome and uninteresting task of mastering the Acts of 1860 and 1870, and of enquiring upon what principles the reforms in these statutes proceeded, and to what extent the previous law, for the better or for the worse, was thereby altered. The enthusiasm of more than one advocate of a reform of the Irish law has been cooled by the discovery that the legal injustice, the supposed existence of which had struck him as a crying wrong, formed no part of the law in question, and he has been hence induced to consider the complaints of the working of the present system as wholly unfounded. It may, therefore, be useful to lay before the public, in a brief and popular form, the leading principles of the existing Irish Land Law; to show how it has grown to be what it is; how it differs from that existing in England; upon what principles these changes have been made; and to draw attention to the points in which the Irish Law, and the Roman and French Law upon this subject, resemble or contradict each other.

It is not the object of this work to propose

any specific alteration or amendment in the existing law. The enquiry what the law is, and how it came to be what it is, is entirely distinct from that whether the existing law should be amended, and if so, in what particulars, and to what extent. It is needless to observe that no rule of law dealing with the contracts of owners and hirers of land is in itself objectively good or bad; the law which is most advantageous in one society would, if suddenly introduced into another, seem unjust, and probably prove mischievous; the good or evil effects of any law depend upon its being applicable or inapplicable to the social condition of the society into which it is introduced. The unreformed English Real Property Law of the fifteenth and sixteenth centuries had become simply intolerable in the nineteenth century; but great as are the evils which arise from the unreasonable retention of an antiquated system, they are not greater than those caused by the introduction, into a comparatively backward community, of laws constructed for a wealthy and progressive society. The question how, and to what extent, the Irish Land Law should be altered involves the consideration of both the present social condition of Ireland and its probable future—a very large and difficult subject, foreign to the objects and outside of the scope of the present work.

CHAPTER I.

CUSTOMARY TENURES.

To avoid the false analogies which upon this subject are frequently drawn from various ancient and modern systems of law, and the reforms which were from time to time effected in them, it is to be observed that all laws defining the rights and duties of landlords and tenants are divisible into two distinct classes, differing altogether in their origin, first principles, and development.

The more ancient systems of law dealing with the present as well as with many other legal relations are purely customary; these are not laws in the technical sense of the term, but simply statements of the manner in which individuals standing in a certain legal relation to each other have hitherto acted, and to which course of action public opinion requires that future members of the community shall conform their conduct. The custom having been reduced to writing and enforced by a sanction, becomes thus in a somewhat circuitous fashion 'law' in the proper sense of the term; such a system of rules when once established may be altered or expanded by an act of the sovereign authority, but it will always retain its essential character, namely, that the reciprocal rights and duties of the landlord and tenant arise by law from the relation in which they stand to each other, and neither spring from nor are referred to any contract previously entered into between the parties, but are fixed and incapable of alteration even by agreement of the parties themselves. Of such a nature was at the commencement of this century the relation of the Prussian noble and peasant,[1] and at a later period that of the Russian boyar and serf, and traces of this ancient system still remain in the English copyhold tenures.

[1] The Prussian peasants owned the peasant-land of an estate by as high a title as the lord held the noble-land of the same; thus the peasants did not hold of the lord, nor was there any relation of contract between them. The lord could not eject a peasant nor remove him from off the estate, nor purchase the holding of a peasant family; because the full number of peasant hearths had to be kept up for the purposes of the conscription. The peasants did not pay rent in the proper sense of the term, but were bound to render their lords certain services, the performance of which was enforced by means other than eviction. What these means were may be easily surmised, if it be remembered that until within the last few years the nobles of Mecklenberg retained the right of flogging their serfs.

The celebrated reform of the Prussian law simply permitted the tenant to compound for the services to which his land was subject, and to continue to hold his own land, or the residue of it, released in future from any feudal obligation.

As customary tenures have always been of exceptional rarity in Ireland, and have within the last few years ceased to exist, we may disregard the first class of tenures known as customary, and turn our attention exclusively to the second or conventional class.

CHAPTER II.

CONVENTIONAL TENURES.

As communities increase in wealth and land acquires a commercial value agriculture becomes a distinct profession, and the possession of land is desired as an ordinary investment of capital. It is obvious that it is more advantageous for the farmer who desires to make profit by agriculture that he should preserve his capital intact and pay for the right to occupy his farm by allotting to the owner of the land a certain proportion of the annual produce, than that he should sink all or a large proportion of his capital in the absolute purchase of an estate. Thus the increasing wealth of a community introduces an entirely new view of the relations between the owner and the occupier of land; the right to occupy and cultivate land is sold like any other marketable article; the owner of the land endeavours to obtain the highest market value, and the tenant strives to make the most advantageous bargain possible. In such a rapidly changing state of society the old rules of land tenure, which represent the original relation of lord and vassal, or freeman and serf, are found inapplicable and inconvenient, and all classes in the community are interested in abolishing the antiquated rules of tenure and permitting the owners of land to let and the tenants to acquire the possession of land upon such terms as they may agree upon between themselves.

In every progressive society the laws relative to the rights and duties of the owner and hirer of land tend to follow an invariable order of change; the parties are permitted to make their own bargains; land may be dealt with as any other commodity; the law ceases to define beforehand by fixed rules what shall be the reciprocal rights of the owner and hirer of land, and leaves to them, within wider or narrower limits, by their contract to determine as between themselves what shall be their respective rights and duties. This alteration in the theory of the relation of landlord and tenant is only one example of the great step in legal development which is technically called the shifting of rights from the basis of status to that of contract. When this change has once taken place the Executive no longer interferes to compel men to act according to certain invariable, and often unintelligible, rules, but to enforce contracts entered into by the parties, who by their mutual stipulations have, in fact, made the law for themselves.

In no contract, whether dealing with land or any other subject-matter, do the parties express *in extenso* all the rights and obligations which flow from the actual terms of their agreement; the vast majority of such rights and obligations are not expressed in the contract itself, but are annexed to it by the law; yet they are regarded as implied terms of the contract; and rightly so, because the parties must be taken to have had regard to them when they entered into their contract, and also because they were at liberty (save in specially excepted cases) to have contracted themselves out of them. The contracts for the hiring of land, which are in ordinary use, are very restricted in number; and the implied terms of the contract being, or being supposed to be, well known, a very short agreement provides for a large number of cases, the specific enumeration of which would be tedious and impossible, the parties being left at liberty, if they object to the implied terms, to substitute others for them by an express contract. If the rights and obligations of the parties are referable to the contract which they have entered into, an obvious difficulty arises if the possession of land has been given to the tenant without any definite contract having been arrived at; it is, therefore, necessary for the law to presume or make a contract for the parties, the terms of which are enforced as if it had in fact been entered into. The discussion of the question what contract the parties ought to have entered into, and into which for the purpose of any action they are to be presumed to have entered into, led the civil lawyers to consider what were the rights and obligations which, in the case of the hiring of land, would have been acquired or incurred by the parties to the transaction, if they had both been honest and intelligent men and had understood the nature of the contract into which they entered. In prosecuting this enquiry the civil lawyers were free from the influence of feudal ideas, and founded their conclusions upon the intrinsic nature of the contract itself and the obvious principles of ethics; and the abstract contract thus developed by them became a model for subsequent legislation; and being specifically embodied in the Code Napoléon, has widely influenced European ideas as to the respective rights of owners and hirers of land. The fairest mode of drawing our attention to the peculiar characteristics of the system of land tenure in Ireland is to compare the provisions of that law with the contract to be implied in the ordinary cases of the hiring of land, as framed by jurists who were perfectly free from that prejudice in favour of landlords which has been transmitted, like an hereditary taint, through the successive generations of English lawyers.

The simplest and best treatise upon the subject written by a French lawyer is the tract of Pothier entitled 'Traité du Contrat de bail à rente,' which has manifestly formed the basis of the sections 1 and 3, book III., chapter viii., of the Code 'Du Contrat de Louage.' The contract for the letting of lands for agriculture or pasture is termed in the French Code 'bail à ferme,' and is treated as a subsection of the chapter dealing with the general contract of hiring ('Du Contrat de Louage').

Pothier defines the 'bail à rente simple' as a contract by which one of the parties lets, and yields possession of, certain land to the other, and covenants for the quiet enjoyment thereof, subject to the reservation of an annual rent, consisting either of a sum certain of money or of a fixed proportion of the annual produce which he retains to himself out of the lands, and which the other reciprocally binds himself to pay so long as he shall enjoy the possession of the lands in question.

The contract regarded from this point of view creates reciprocal duties and rights; the rights of the landlord are the complement of the tenant's duties; and further, neither party can claim his rights unless and until he fulfil his duties.

The full enjoyment by the tenant of the lands demised is a condition antecedent to the right of the landlord to require the payment of his rent, and the tenant has not any right to continue in the possession of the premises unless he pay the rent. Whatever, therefore, be the date of the contract, the reciprocal duties created thereby do not come into operation until the tenant is put into possession of the premises demised.

By the contract the lessor is supposed to transfer to the lessee the ownership ('la propriété') in the premises subject to a charge of the rent upon the interest of the lessee; the rent is primarily a charge upon the lessee's interest, and the lessee personally bound to pay it only so long as he remain in actual possession; and the obligation to pay the rent ceases if the lessee be deprived of the enjoyment of the premises.

The duties of the lessor are stated thus, to put the lessee into possession and to guarantee him the quiet possession of the premises demised; those of the tenant to pay the rent, to treat the premises in a husbandlike manner, and to surrender the premises at the end of the term in the condition in which he himself had received them.

The theory of the French civilians as to the nature and recovery of rent is the point in which they are most at variance with English ideas. Their views on this matter can only be understood if two points are steadily borne in mind, viz., (1) that a 'bail à ferme' partook of the nature of a sale as well as of a hiring, a question discussed by the Roman lawyers (Justinian's 'Institutes,' iii. 24). Under this apparently verbal discussion there lurks, as is often the case, a question of importance. If a lease be considered as a sale of the lands for a greater or less period, the consideration being not a sum of money but an annuity of equivalent duration and charged upon the lands demised, the court must take into consideration all equities which could be relied upon by a defendant resisting the specific performance of a contract of sale. If a vendor induced a purchaser to give so disproportionately large a price, or a purchaser induced a vendor to accept so absurdly small a price that the disparity of the price itself was evidence of fraud, the civil law would refuse specific performance of the contract; so if the rent reserved in a lease was so much in excess of the value as to be evidence of fraud, the court would allow the lessor to recover only the fair value of the premises: 'Pareillement, de même que la bonne foi ne permet pas au vendeur de vendre au-delà du juste prix, elle ne permet pas non plus au bailleur d'imposer par le bail la charge d'une rente trop forte qui excède le juste prix.' This principle was equally applicable to the case of the lessee : 'Le bail à rente étant un contrat commutatif où chacune des parties entend recevoir autant qu'elle donne, la bonne foi oblige le preneur de se charger par le bail d'une rente qui ne soit pas au-dessous de la juste valeur de la propriété de l'héritage qui lui est transféré par le bail.' It is not to be understood that in an ordinary case the court enquired as to the actual value of the premises, and fixed the rent at that amount disregarding the terms of the contract; in case of extraordinary and disproportionate excess, a disproportion produced by or in itself evidence of fraud, it disregarded the fraudulent rent and treated the case as an action for use and occupation. That this is the correct construction to be placed upon this passage of Pothier is shown by the following extract from the work of Merlin, who wrote with the treatise of Pothier before him: 'Quand le prix du bail n'égalerait pas la valeur de la jouissance de la chose louée, la convention n'en aurait pas moins tout son effet. En cela le contrat de louage diffère de celui de vente. On sait que le vendeur peut faire rescinder la vente lorsqu'elle a été faite pour une somme au-dessous de la moitié du juste prix.'

'Mais de quelque considération que soit la lésion dans le contrat à louage, elle ne peut pas le faire résoudre, à moins qu'elle ne soit accompagnée de quelques circonstances particulières, telles que le dol ou l'erreur. La raison en est que l'incertitude de la valeur des revenues des temps à venir peut mettre un juste équilibre entre la condition du bailleur et celle du preneur.'[1]

If the rent reserved upon a contract for the letting of land had continued to be what in early times it was, a fixed proportion of the gross produce of the land, the rent which the lessor would have received must have varied with the greater or less abundance of the harvest. The lessor and lessee were at first practically partners in the crop, the lessor supplying the land and the lessee the labour. When the lessor commuted

[1] Sub v. Baux, tom. 1, fol. 707.

his fixed proportion of the crop into a fixed annual payment two equitable rules were introduced: (1) that the landlord should be taken to have covenanted that the annual produce would exceed the rent, and (2) that if the crop failed by any unforeseen cause the lessor should share the loss with the lessee. The application of this principle will appear in the subsequent extracts from the French Code. The mode in which the rent might be recovered was determined by the standpoint from which the nature of the rent was regarded. Rent might be considered as either (1) an annual sum which the tenant had contracted to pay as the consideration for the possession of the lands, or (2) as an annuity charged upon the interest of the tenant in the lands, or (3) as the share of the landlord in the annual produce of the lands, or (4) as a sum of money the payment of which was a condition precedent to the tenant's right of occupation.

The landlord had, therefore, a personal action not only against the tenant and his heirs, but also against third parties in possession who had acquired it with notice of the existence of the rent, and against their heirs for the recovery of the arrears of the rent which accrued during their possession or that of their ancestors. As to the arrears of rent which had accrued prior to the purchase of the tenant's interest by an assignee in possession, the landlord had no personal action against the assignee, but he could proceed to recover all arrears by an 'hypothecary' action; that is, he could treat the arrears of rent as a charge upon the tenant's interest, and raise them by a sale of the interest, as if he were a mortgagee for that amount. 'Cette action naît de l'affectation de l'héritage au payement de ces arrérages. L'héritage sujet à la rente foncière étant proprement le débiteur de la rente dont il est chargé, c'est une suite qu'il soit affecté au payement de tous les arrérages qui en sont dus.'

The landlord had further a right, similar to the hypothec of the Scotch law, to treat the produce of the lands and property upon the lands as specifically pledged to him for the payment of the rent. When the tenant, personally liable to the payment of the rent, was himself in possession, the landlord possessed a very stringent power of thus recovering his rent, which was defined—' une espèce de droit de gage sur les fruits nés de l'héritage chargé de la rente, et sur les meubles qui en occupent les logis, lequel droit se perd lorsque les choses ont été transportées hors de l'héritage, si le créancier n'en a pas poursuivi le rétablissement dans le court délai qui lui est accordé. Ce droit, de même que celui du locateur, s'étend à tous les meubles qui servent à l'exploitation de la maison ou métairie sujette à la rente foncière, quand même ils n'appartiendraient pas au débiteur de la rente. C'est aussi une suite de ce droit que, lorsque les fruits et les meubles qui étaient dans l'héritage sujet à la rente en ont été déplacés, le seigneur de rente foncière a, comme les locateurs de maisons et métairies, le droit de les suivre et de les faire rétablir pour sa sûreté.'

If the farm had been sublet, the right of the landlord did not attach upon the crops or the goods of the subtenant, but upon the interest in the lands of the tenant, namely, the rent payable under the subletting. It is necessary to observe that the right to treat the produce of the farm as charged with the rent is entirely different in its origin from the right of distress given to landlords by the English law. If the tenant failed to perform any of the obligations, the fulfilment of which was the condition upon which he was entitled to the possession, his interest in the lands necessarily determined. This result followed not merely from the breach of express stipulations, such as an express agreement to build and improve, but also from implied covenants, as, for example, for the payment of rent and the proper cultivation of the land. The interest of the tenant was not, however, summarily determined, as upon a proviso for re-entry upon breach of covenants in an English lease; the judgment of a court was requisite to declare the tenant's interest forfeited. Courts which followed the equitable principles of the Roman law were not likely to determine the tenant's interest unless the breach of covenants had been substantial and wilful, nor without giving the tenant an opportunity of fulfilling his obligations. Thus, in the case of the action brought by the landlord seeking not merely payment of his rent, but also an ejectment for non-payment of rent ('pour rentrer dans l'héritage à défaut de paiement'), it is observed, 'A l'égard de l'autre objet de l'action, qui est de rentrer dans l'héritage à défaut de paiement de la rente, le bailleur n'y est reçu que lorsqu'il lui est dû *plusieurs termes;* même en ce cas le juge, avant de statuer définitivement, a coutume d'ordonner que le preneur sera tenu de payer dans un certain temps, fixé par la sentence, faute de quoi il sera permis au bailleur de rentrer.' If the tenant paid rent and costs within the time limited, he could dismiss the action and *remain* in the farm. Whatever was the judgment, the action being essentially for the recovery of rent, he could pay the rent and costs at any time before execution and the re-entry of the landlord; but after such execution and re-entry the tenant had no further time to redeem ('il ne seroit plus à temps d'offrir le paiement des arrérages'). The right of the landlord being to secure the payment of his rent, or for this purpose to determine the tenancy, he was entitled to recover the farm in the same state as it was when originally let. In such a case the tenant also was entitled to the value of his improvements (*améliorations*), and an account was settled, in which he was credited with their value and debited with the rent. The re-entry of the landlord did not extinguish the personal liability of the tenant to pay the arrears, a rule inconsistent with the theory that the tenant's interest in the lands was the primary security.

In the absence of express agreement, a contract on the part of the tenant was implied that he would till the ground in a husbandlike manner, and keep all buildings, &c., in proper repair; and the failure to perform these duties involved a forfeiture of his interest, and liability to the damages 'résultant de ce que l'héritage vaut moins que la rente par les dégradations qu'il y a faites.' This claim of the tenant for compensation for improvements upon the re-entry of the landlord under a judgment in an action for non-payment of rent arises from the fact that the landlord, by the form of the action which he has selected, determines the tenancy before the period appointed for its regular effluxion. If the legal relations of landlord and tenant are referred exclusively to contract, a tenant who gives up the possession at the end of his term can have no claim for compensation for improvements if he be merely required to give up the land in the same condition as that in which he received it; but if a landlord himself determines an interest of uncertain duration, or one of certain duration, before the date fixed for its termination, the claim of the tenant for compensation for his improvements is an obvious equity.

This distinction is clearly taken in the Brehon law tract known as the breatha comaitcheasa andso

'If the land has been let for hire, and no time has been specified, whatever length of time he shall be upon it, whether with necessity or without necessity he goes, he shall leave behind the erections. If he be noticed to quit, whether it is done with or without necessity, he may carry away his erections with him. If a term has been specified, and the term has expired, he shall leave his erections behind.'—*Ancient Laws of Ireland,* vol. IV. pp. 132-133.

CHAPTER III.

THE CODE NAPOLÉON.

THE Code Napoléon is not an exhaustive treatise—merely an outline statement of the broad principles of law applicable to certain legal relations; the sections dealing with the relation of landlord and tenant lay down wide general principles leaving the application of them to the executive, and avoiding any reference to forms of procedure. In the Code the letting of land is treated as falling under the ordinary contract of hiring ('louage'), and the rights and duties of both parties as implied from the contract into which they have entered. A few brief extracts will show that the principles of the Code are almost identical with those of Pothier. The obligations of the landlord (bailleur) are briefly defined: 'Le bailleur est, par la nature du contrat, et sans qu'il soit besoin d'aucune convention particulière, tenu des trois obligations suivantes: (1) Il doit délivrer au preneur la chose louée, et cela en bon état de réparation de toute espèce. (2) Le bailleur doit entretenir la chose louée en état de servir à l'usage auquel elle est destinée, et par conséquence il doit y faire toutes les réparations qui peuvent devenir nécessaires. Les obligations du bailleur et du preneur sont *successives;* le bailleur n'acquiert le droit au prix du louage qu'au fur et à mesure qu'il procure au preneur la jouissance de la chose louée. (3) Le bailleur est tenu de faire jouir paisiblement le preneur de la chose louée.'

As to the obligations of the tenant they are as follows : ' Le preneur est tenu de deux obligations principales: (1) De payer le prix du bail aux termes convenus. (2) D'user de la chose louée en bon père de famille ; le preneur devant user de la chose louée en bon père de famille, il est évident qu'il répond des dégradations et des pertes arrivées pendant sa jouissance, soit par son fait, soit par le fait des personnes de sa maison, de ses sous-locataires, ou de ses concessionaires. Le prêteur devant user de la chose suivant la destination des parties, le bailleur peut, en cas de violation de cette obligation, conclure soit des dommages et intérêts, soit suivant la gravité des circonstances à la résiliation du bail.' The right of the landlord to re-enter for a breach of contract is not therefore absolute, but depends upon the actual injury arising from the breach, and may be resisted upon equitable grounds.

It is distinctly laid down that the letting is determined ' par défaut du bailleur ou du preneur de satisfaire à ses engagements.'

If the lands demised exceed or fall short of the supposed quantity the rent is to be proportionately increased or diminished.

The principle that the tenant forfeits his interest if he fail to fulfil the covenants implied from the nature of the contract is carried to the utmost in the following passage: 'Le preneur d'un bien rural doit le garnir de bestiaux et d'ustensiles nécessaires à son exploitation, sinon il peut être expulsé : il ne serait pas admis à donner d'autres sûretés du payment des fermages, car les bestiaux et les ustensiles sont exigés non seulement comme sûreté du payment des fermages, mais comme garantie d'une bonne culture. Le preneur peut encore être expulsé s'il abandonne la culture, s'il ne cultive pas en bon père de famille, s'il emploie la chose louée à un autre usage que celui auquel elle est destinée, ou, en général, s'il n'exécute pas les clauses du bail, et qu'il résulte de là un dommage grave pour le bailleur. En cas de résiliation provenant d'un fait quelconque de preneur, celui-ci est tenu de dommages et intérêts.'

The obligation of the landlord to share in the loss arising from the crop is based upon the implied contract of the landlord to guarantee that the farm let is what is technically termed 'une possession utile.' The obligation to share in the loss does not, however, arise, unless the deficiency of the crop exceeds one-half of an average harvest; and in the case of a letting for a term of years, the tenant to obtain a reduction of his rent must extend the account over the entire period of the letting, and prove a loss of more than half of the ordinary crop, taking both good and bad years into account.[1]

The tenant, upon giving up the farm, must leave it in the same condition as he received it in. 'Le fermier sortant doit laisser à celui qui lui succède dans la culture les logements convenables et autres facilités pour les travaux de l'année suivante. Le fermier doit laisser les pailles et engrais de l'année, s'il les a reçus à son entrée en jouissance ; s'il ne les a pas reçus, le propriétaire peut les retenir sur estimation, car il a un droit fondé en raison à ce que ses terres ne soient point appauvries.'

If a tenant be put into possession of land under a contract in which the term or duration of the tenancy is not stated, it is necessary for the court to supply this defect in the agreement. The duration of a letting cannot be logically deduced from the nature of the contract. The contract of hiring or letting land is essentially the same whether the term is one or a thousand years. The duration of the letting is to be inferred from the surrounding circumstances and the object with which the land was taken by the lessee.

---

[1] It is clear that as an account is to be taken of profit or loss for the entire term, this rule is inapplicable to a lease for ever; and in the case of an Irish tenancy from year to year, in which the landlord cannot evict the tenant without compensation for disturbance, it may be suggested that the tenure as between parties is of a quasi-perpetual nature, and would not therefore fall, as has been suggested by some, within the equity of this principle.

In the case of an agricultural lease (*d'un fonds rural*) the duration of the letting is fixed by the time required to get in a harvest of the crop usually cultivated upon the lands in question. In the case of corn-land, vineyards, &c., such a letting would be equivalent to one for a year certain; but if the crop to be planted by the tenant is not an annual produce, but of a longer duration, the letting is for as many years as there are seasons of the crop.

CHAPTER IV.

THE FRENCH LAW AS TO 'AMÉLIORATION.'

It has been already stated that neither the Civil [1] nor the French law recognised any right of a tenant for a fixed term to compensation for improvements; he was simply bound to restore the lands in the state in which himself had re-

---

[1] Under the head of *accession*, Mr. Hunter, in his volume upon Roman Law, page 132, treats the case of a contract for hiring, as creating an important exception to the general rule 'omne quod ædificatur solo cedit,' and as his authority refers to three passages in the Digest, which however support his statement to but a limited extent. The first passage (D. 19, 2, 19, 4) amounts to no more than the statement that during the tenancy the tenant could remove fixtures. The second (D. 19, 2, 55, 1) deals with the case of a tenant whose tenancy had been determined by the act of the landlord, and the rule agrees precisely in principle with the passage of Pothier before referred to. The third passage (D. 19, 2, 61, 2) deals with the case of a tenancy in which the landlord was entitled to receive as rent a proportion of the produce, and the tenant by improvements, which he was not bound to make, had caused the lands to produce an *extraordinary* annual crop.

In the two latter cases the nature of the tenant's right is indicated by the nature of his legal remedy. In case No. 2 he might proceed against the landlord in an action 'ex conducto' to recover his expenditure; in the case of No. 3 he might defend himself against the landlord claiming a proportionate share of the gross produce of an 'exceptio doli mali.'

ceived them. The tenant under the Roman law, not specifically as a tenant, but as one of the class of those who were entitled to the possession of the land for a limited period, was practically secured compensation for certain improvements by the rule which permitted him to remove such as were capable of removal, and thus to compel the proprietor to purchase such as were of practical value. The mode in which this result was arrived at cannot be more clearly stated than in the words of Mons. Lesenne: 'Quand le maître des matériaux a bâti *sciemment* sur le fonds d'autrui rigoureusement il en perd pour toujours la propriété, parce qu'il est censé les avoir gratuitement aliénés au profit du maître du terrain, qu'il est d'ailleurs en faute d'avoir témérairement bâti sur un sol qu'il savait n'être pas à lui, et il n'a aucune action ni exception pour se faire indemniser ou reprendre les matériaux, soit qu'il possède, soit qu'il ne possède pas le terrain. Telle est la rigueur du principe exposé dans les Institutes ; mais cette sévérité avait été adoucie dès avant Justinien par diverses décisions des jurisconsultes et des empereurs, qui permettent au constructeur de mauvaise foi de revendiquer ses matériaux après la démolition, s'il n'est prouvé qu'il ait bâti " *donandi animo*," qui obligent le propriétaire, revendiquant le fonds, à indemniser ce constructeur des dépenses nécessaires qu'il a faites, et qui accordent à ce dernier l'exception de dol, si le propriétaire ne lui laisse pas enlever tout ce qui peut l'être sans dégradation, ou ne lui en offre pas la valeur véniale' (*De La Propriété*, &c., sect. 99). Questions as to improvements by a tenant are considered by the French lawyers from a point of view different from that in which we are accustomed to regard them. Such questions are argued by us with the object of deciding whether the tenant should be compensated for his improvements; by the French lawyers with the object of deciding whether the tenant should be bound to restore the lands to their original condition. Such questions, therefore, are not treated in the Code under the head of the hiring of land, but as specific instances to which should be applied the general principles of *accession*, that is, the rules which deal with the case of the properties of two individuals having been inextricably intermingled by the act of one of them. The general rule upon this subject is very fully set out in the 555th section of the Code Civil: 'Lorsque les plantations, constructions, ouvrages ont été faits par un tiers et avec ses matériaux, le propriétaire du fonds a droit ou de les retenir, ou d'obliger ce tiers à les enlever. Si le propriétaire du fonds demande la suppression des plantations et constructions, celle-ci est aux frais de celui qui les a faites, sans aucune indemnité pour lui; il peut même être condamné à des dommages et intérêts, s'il y a lieu, pour le préjudice que peut avoir éprouvé le propriétaire du fonds. Si le propriétaire préfère conserver les plantations et constructions, il doit le remboursement de la valeur des matériaux et du prix de la main-d'œuvre sans égard à la plus ou moins augmentation de valeur que le fonds a pu recevoir. Néanmoins, si les plantations et constructions et ouvrages ont été faits par un tiers évincé, qui l'aurait condamné à la restitution des fonds, attendu sa bonne foi, le propriétaire ne pourra demander la suppression desdits ouvrages, plantations, et constructions, mais il aura le choix ou de rembourser la valeur des matériaux et du prix de la main-d'œuvre, ou de rembourser une somme égale à celle dont le fonds a augmenté de valeur.'

The rights of the person who has made the improvements depend upon the question whether they have been made in good or in bad faith; they are made in good faith when the person who made them believed that he himself was the proprietor; in bad faith when he knew, or ought to have known, that he was not so. Hence it has been decided by the French Courts that a person himself entitled to a terminable interest in the land, under which head a 'fermier' is included, must be held to have made the improvements 'de mauvaise foi';[1] and that therefore upon the determination of a tenancy the landlord is entitled to elect whether he would take the improvements of the tenant at their original cost, irrespective of the increased value of the farm, or require the

[1] Lesenne, *De la Propriété*, &c., p. 243.

outgoing tenant to restore the lands to their original condition. The Canadian Code, which is merely a translation of the Code Civil, contains the 555th section of the French Code as section No. 417, and to prevent any mistake as to its meaning, gives, in section No. 412, an express definition of the term 'in good faith,' in accordance with the previous decisions of the French Courts above referred to.

The principles of the Law of Landlord and Tenant adopted in the Code Napoléon are almost the same established by the Roman, but the latter does not in the Institutes group them together in any single chapter, and they are throughout the work scattered under different heads,[1] but a comparison of the French Code with the analysis of the Roman Law upon the subject contained in Hunter's Roman Law will at once establish their identity.[2]

---

[1] The Roman decisions and authorities on the subject are collected in the 19th Book of the Digest.

[2] This right of the landlord to require the tenant, upon the termination of the letting, to restore the premises to their original condition, by the removal of useless, or mischievous *improvements*, is of considerable importance, and may be illustrated by the following:—A tenant holding the estate of the Skinners' Company for the residue of a long term of 99 years, commenced to build thereon an enormous mansion, which at the termination of the lease was left unfinished and in a ruinous condition. In a suit to administer the assets of the tenant, a claim was brought in by the Company for waste, and one of the points relied upon was the partial erection and subsequent abandonment of the house in

question. Upon this point the claim failed, because the building of the house, although never completed, was what the English law defines as 'ameliorating waste,' and the tenant was not bound by any covenant to complete or keep it in repair. (Scott *v.* Ogilvie, *M. of R. unreported*).

CHAPTER V.

LEADING PRINCIPLES OF THE FRENCH LAW.

The Roman Law of landlord and tenant as codified by the French is a system thoroughly consequent and logical; if the first principles upon which it is founded are once admitted, it is impossible not to admit its most extreme conclusions. The system rests upon the following assumptions:

(1.) That there should be free trade in land, and that the rules as to the hiring of land should be the same as those applicable to the hiring of any other commodity;

(2.) That the relative rights and obligations of a landlord and his tenant are solely derived from the contract into which they have entered;

(3.) That in default of any express agreement, and so far as their agreement is silent, their rights and obligations are such as equity would infer from the nature of the contract itself;

(4.) That the rights and obligations of the landlord and tenant are strictly reciprocal;

(5.) That neither the landlord nor tenant can claim the benefit of the contract unless he himself has previously fulfilled his obligations.

The French law is based upon the application to the landlord and tenant, with the utmost impartiality, of the same general propositions; if it gives no undue advantage to the landlord, it certainly does not favour the tenant; it refuses to regard the relation of landlord and tenant as anything exceptional, and applies to their rights and obligations the same principles and regards them in the same spirit as it would those of the owner and hirer of the most ordinary article; it is the most complete and equitable application of the rules of free trade to the case of the letting and hiring of land.

CHAPTER VI.

THE ENGLISH LANDLORD AND TENANT LAW AS SUBSISTING IN IRELAND PRIOR TO 1860.

THE English law upon this subject is, like much else of English law, inconsequent and illogical; it consists of a vast and undigested mass of statutes and legal decisions, piled up without any leading principle or definite ideas. Commencing at a period when the landlord was all-powerful and the tenant's rights wholly disregarded, it has been continually amended in favour of the tenant, so much so that it is a question whether even the English Law as it now exists (or the Irish Law as it stood before 1860) is not more beneficial for the tenant than the Roman or French Law, and whether the rights of the landlord would not be vastly increased by the introduction into England of the Code Napoléon.

The lettings of lands in Ireland prior to the year 1870 may for the present purpose be divided into three classes, viz., (A.) Leases, (B.) Yearly tenancies, and (C.) Tenancies at will.

(A.) In the case of a lease the landlord by a deed granted the land in question to the tenant either for lives, or for years (it is immaterial for the present purpose whether a lease was freehold or not), subject to the payment of the rent agreed upon, and the tenant on his part covenanted to pay the rent and to do or forbear from doing such other acts as had been agreed upon between the parties; the lease generally contained a further proviso that if the tenant violated any of the covenants entered into by him, the landlord could re-enter and determine the estate of the tenant. The effect of such a proviso was to place the tenant in the same position as to the payment of rent and the fulfilment of covenants as the French Law considers every tenant to stand in without any express covenant.

(B.) Yearly tenancies or tenancies from year to year appear to have first arisen in the 16th century, and the validity of this fashion of letting was established as the result of Potkyns case, 14 Hen. VIII. In this original case it is described as a 'lease for the term of a year to commence at Michaelmas and continue unto the end of the said year, and so on to the next year, de anno in annum, as long as the parties pleased.' In ordinary language the letting was for an indefinite term of years commencing at a fixed date and determinable at the end of any current year by either party upon service of a six months' notice.'

---

¹ Lettings of land in Ireland for agricultural or pastoral purposes, by which tenancies from year to year were created subsequently to the 15th August, 1876, are now to be determinable upon a twelve months' notice to quit on any gale

This mode of tenure suited the views of the owners of lands—then more anxious to secure political influence than to improve their estates—when the suffrage, previously confined to leaseholds, was in 1850, by the Act of the 13-14 Vict., ch. 69, extended to the occupiers of land of the annual rating of 12*l*.

A tenancy from year to year might exist for generations, and thus in the ideas of the tenants it was regarded as an almost perpetual interest, although subject at any time to be determined by a notice to quit; at an early period of the Common Law it would probably have developed into a perpetual customary tenure, as was the case of the copyhold tenure in England.

(C.) A tenancy at will was a letting of land for such period as both landlord and tenant chose that the relation between them should continue—practically, so long as the landlord chose. But lands were very rarely held upon these terms, as such tenures could then be created only by special agreement.

In the case of a letting which did not specify the term for which the lands were held, the English Courts had to decide what term was to be implied in the contract, or inferred from the fact that the occupier was found in possession paying

day of the calendar year, in which the rent becomes due and payable, irrespective of the period of the year at which the tenancy commenced; and for certain specific purposes notice to quit may be served as to portion only of the holding. 39, 40 Vic., ch. 63.

rent to the owner. This question was solved, as a matter of fact, by the assumption that the letting was similar to that in most ordinary use at the time; down to the time of Lord Mansfield, the presumption was that the tenancy was one at will: from his date it was a tenancy from year to year.

It is useful now to consider what were the chief rights and obligations, other than by express agreement, of landlords and tenants in the same order as that in which they are dealt with in the French Code.

As to the landlord's implied obligations. (1) He did not guarantee to the tenant that he had good title to make the lease, and therefore, if the tenant were put out of possession by the true owner of the land, he had no remedy against the landlord; (2) he was not bound to keep the premises in repair; (3) he did not guarantee to the tenant what the French lawyers defined as a 'possession utile.'

The rights and obligations of the tenant, other than by express contract, were as follows: (1) He was bound to pay the rent reserved; (2) he was prohibited from committing waste, that is, destroying the subject matter by pulling down buildings, &c.; (3) he was bound to give up possession at the termination of the lettings; (4) he was not bound to keep the premises in repair; (5) he was not bound to cultivate the premises '*en bon père de famille;*' (6) he was not bound to give them up in as good condition as he received them.

The tenant was entitled, as any other owner of an interest in land, to sell or sublet his farm to whom and upon what terms he pleased. It is frequently assumed that, in the case of a tenancy from year to year, the tenant had no such right, and the mistake may have arisen in the following manner. The tenant could convey to a purchaser no more than he himself had, and, upon the sale of a tenancy from year to year, the landlord, if he had any objection to the purchaser, could determine the yearly tenancy by a notice to quit, and owners of land are, as a matter of fact, unwilling to have a new tenant forced upon them of whose character and solvency they are ignorant; the purchaser, therefore, as a matter of precaution, required an assurance from the landlord that he was willing to accept him as a substitute for the former tenant; but whether the landlord assented or not to the sale, all the interest of the previous tenant passed by the sale to the purchaser.

The tenant who held land for a period of uncertain duration had a right to the annual industrial crops upon the lands at the determination of his letting, and to return into the farm for the purpose of harvesting and removing them; this was technically termed his right of emblements.

As to the recovery of the rent, and the enforcement of covenants or agreements entered into by the tenant, the payment and fulfilment of these was not a condition precedent upon which the tenant was entitled to retain the possession; and his interest was not forfeited by the non-payment or non-fulfilment of them.[1]

The law did not regard the relation of landlord and tenant as a quasi-partnership (société), nor did it treat the rent as the landlord's share in the produce of the farm. Hence the rent was not a charge upon the tenant's interest by way of hypothec; nor were the crops considered as pledged for its payment, nor was the landlord's rent subject to deductions on account of the loss of the crop.

The modes of enforcing the payment of the rent were three:—

(I.) A personal action might be brought against the tenant either founded upon his express contract, or upon the implied contract arising from his occupation.

(II.) For a long period the English law regarded the proceeding of distress as the ordinary mode of compelling the payment of rent. A distress was originally used to enforce the performance of feudal obligations, not the payment

---

[1] The difference between the English and French law upon this subject arose from the fact that the latter referred the *possession* of the tenant solely to the contract of hiring; the former considered the tenant to have acquired an actual *estate* in the lands for the term specified in an antecedent agreement.

of money, and the rights of the lord had been restricted by the statute of Marlbridge to the bare power of seizing the goods on the premises and retaining them as a pledge until the services were performed. But when the process of distress was applied to the recovery of a money rent, the right of the landlord was extended to that of selling the goods seized, and retaining the arrears of rent out of the produce. Proceedings by distress required the performance of so many technical forms, introduced for the benefit of the tenant, and the failure to comply with these legal technicalities, by rendering the whole proceeding illegal *ab initio*, exposed the landlord to such heavy damages that a proceeding by distress for the recovery of rent was always most reluctantly adopted.[1]

[1] The discredit into which the process of recovering rent by distress gradually fell is illustrated by the General Orders of the Irish Court of Chancery for the management of estates by the Receivers. By the 2nd G. O. of the 5th April, 1847, a Receiver was empowered, when the rent had remained unpaid for a certain time, to proceed by distress for the recovery of such rent without any Rule or Order for that purpose, *such remedy to be deemed a proper one in the first instance;* but he could not proceed either in the Superior or County Court for the recovery of the rent without the direction of the Master. The 22nd G. O. of the 19th of May, 1857, amended the former by striking out therefrom the provision that the remedy by distress should be deemed the proper one to be taken by the Receiver for the recovery of rent in arrear, in the first instance, and directing that civil bill proceedings, where suitable, should be substituted in lieu thereof.

(III.) The action of ejectment, an action to recover the possession of land, could originally only be brought for non-payment of rent, when the letting was by a lease which contained a clause allowing the landlord to re-enter and avoid the lease upon the non-fulfilment by the tenant of his covenant to pay the rent. The right to recover in the action rested, not upon the non-payment of the rent, but upon the determination of the letting. Previous to 1851 the right to bring an ejectment when one whole year's rent had been in arrear was extended to all cases of lettings under a written agreement, whether it did or did not contain a clause of re-entry, but was not applicable to the most numerous case of implied tenancies from year to year not created by a written agreement, but arising from the fact of the payment of rent.[1] The landlord in the latter case could not eject the tenant for non-payment of rent, but was forced to serve a notice to quit determining the tenancy; hence, if A on January 1, 1840, let land to B as a yearly tenant without writing, and B failed to pay the second and third half-yearly gales, which fell due on December 31, 1840, and June 30, 1841, A would have had to serve him with a notice to quit for January 1, 1843, and might thus have lost two and one half-years' rent before he could recover possession. To remedy

[1] 5 Geo. II., ch. 4, s. 1 (Irish); and 25 Geo. II., ch. 13, s. 2 (Irish.)

this evil the right to bring an ejectment in the Civil Bill Courts upon non-payment of one year's rent was given to landlords, in the case of holdings at a rent of less than 50*l*. per annum not held under a written agreement, by the 14 and 15 Vict. c. 57, s. 73, but the tenancies of a higher amount remained subject to the old rule.

The Courts of Equity regarded the proviso for re-entry and forfeiture as merely a mode of securing the payment of the rent, and if, therefore, the tenant within a reasonable time (limited by statute to six months) paid the arrears of rent he could file a bill in Chancery to redeem his interest, and upon the settlement of an account between him and the landlord, in which the latter was charged with so much as he could in the interval without wilful default have made out of the premises, the forfeited lease was reinstated and the tenant put back into possession. This process of redemption was carried out in the manner most inconvenient to both parties; the tenant was put out of possession, and thus his means of paying the rent seriously diminished, and the landlord was put into possession of lands of which for six months he could make no profitable use; and as if the more to embarrass the landlord the mortgagees of the tenant had, it is difficult to see why, three further months during which they might themselves redeem.

From the state of the real property law the person who ordinarily received the rent, and acted as the owner of the estate, might not be legally entitled to take any proceedings against the tenant; the right to the rent, as it was technically described, ran with the reversion—that is, in the theory of law, the relation of landlord and tenant did not arise unless the landlord was, as a matter of fact, entitled at law to the possession of the premises demised upon the natural determination of the lease. Thus, if A, entitled to the land for twenty years from January 1, 1840, let these lands to B for ten years from January 1, 1850, the relation of landlord and tenant did not arise, but it would have arisen if he had let them for ten years from December 31, 1849. To the person who, claiming through the original landlord, was entitled to the possession of the lands on the determination of the lease the rights of the landlord as against the tenant passed. In most cases the person entitled to the 'reversion' was a mortgagee, or trustee, or some other who had no practical connection with the business in hand or knowledge of the estate. Hence most actions against tenants had to be brought in the names of those who were strangers to the estates, and were naturally unwilling to have anything to say to the matter. As the interest of the tenant frequently was dealt with in the same manner as that of the landlord, it was often the case that when the *technical* landlord had been discovered it was equally difficult to discover the *technical* tenant. The legal subtleties formerly in use to escape the difficulties created by equally absurd anterior legal subtleties are now happily forgotten; but it can be easily understood that the probability that in a proceeding against a tenant the action would be defeated by some wholly immaterial and purely technical point rendered those in receipt of the rents timorous of instituting actions, and afforded to the tenant a questionable protection. Every improvement in the real property law has been injurious to the tenants; to a man in possession, a defendant in ejection, no system of law is so advantageous as one hopelessly entangled and incomprehensible.

Upon the determination of the letting, the tenant gave up the land as it stood, and the landlord took it up as it stood. If the tenant lost his improvements, the landlord might have thrown back on his hands a farm almost worthless from wasteful cultivation; the inequities were in theory balanced, but in practice the rule told against the tenant.[1] The wilful running out of the land so injurious to the owner frequently occurred in the case of tenants for fixed terms, but did not so often arise in the case of yearly

---

[1] This passage is fully justified by the expressions of Baron Parke in 'Hutton *v.* Warren' (1 Mee & Welsb, 466): 'The Common Law, indeed, does so little to prescribe the relative duties of landlord and tenant, since *it leaves the latter at liberty to pursue any course of management he pleases, provided that he is not guilty of waste*, that,' &c.

tenants who expected to hold on their farms. In the latter case it was always in the power of the landlord, if a tenant improved his farm, to serve a notice to quit, and having got rid of his tenant and appropriated his improvements to relet to another at a higher rate. Hence the notice to quit was frequently used as an unjust means of raising the rent, inasmuch as the tenant was thus compelled either to abandon his improvements to the landlord, or to consent to pay a rent increased by reason of the increased value which he himself had given to the farm—such a proceeding on the part of the landlord is what Pothier condemns as contrary to the rule of equity, 'qui ne permet pas de s'enrichir aux dépens d'autrui.'

The principle of law laid down by Gaius, ' id quod in solo nostro ab aliquo ædificatum est, quamvis ille suo nomine ædificaverit, jure naturali nostrum fit, quia superficies solo cedit' (L. II. s. 73), was adopted by the English law, but without the equitable exception annexed to the rule by the Roman Code. The English rule as to fixtures had not its origin in any feudal custom, although it, like every objectionable portion of the landlord and tenant law, is popularly referred to the 'feudal system.' Like many other principles of the Roman it was, without any legislative authority, considered as portion of the English law upon the authority of Bracton, who copied into his work De Legibus, &c., Angliæ, passages of the Institutes and Digest without acknowledgment. It was the incompleteness of Bracton's statement of the rule of the Roman Law (Brac. l. 2, c. 1, s. 4) which rendered the English law so rigid and inequitable. Hence anything *annexed* by the tenant to the premises became a fixture and part of the substance of the freehold; he had therefore no greater interest in it than he had in the premises themselves, and would be guilty of waste if he removed it. The strictness of the law had been relaxed in favour of trade and manufacture, and also as to articles of ornament and personal convenience; but the question of fixtures remained a fertile subject of litigation, and the law reports contained learned judgments upon the rights of the landlord and tenant as to gas pipes, grates, water-butts, pumps, bells, pier-glasses, hothouses, &c.[1]

---

[1] The distinctions drawn by the French Law as between 'biens immeubles' and 'biens meubles' are just as refined. No rule of English law as to 'constructive fixtures' exceeds the following: 'Quant aux statues, elles sont immeubles lorsqu' elles sont placées dans une niche *pratiquée exprès pour les recevoir*, encore qu' elles puissent être enlevées sans fracture ou détérioration.' Code Civil, s. 525.

CHAPTER VII.

THE LANDLORD AND TENANT ACT 1860.

THE law of landlord and tenant both in England and Ireland being in this most chaotic and illogical condition, an attempt was made in Ireland in 1860 to remedy its most glaring defects and to introduce some intelligible rules suitable to the existing state of society. It is easy to perceive why this reform was attempted in Ireland, but has not yet been introduced into England.

Political economists universally asserted that the wretched condition of Ireland arose from the embarrassed circumstances and want of business habits of the Irish landowners. 'Substitute' they said, ' for the present landlords, practical men of business who will invest their capital in the purchase of Irish estates, and deal with the property which they so acquire in a thoroughly commercial spirit; the true interests of the landlords and tenants are identical, and for his own benefit an intelligent landlord must improve the condition of his tenantry.' Thirty years since the political economists were the prophets of the period, and it was the received doctrine that free trade in land and the purchase of land to be dealt with as a commercial speculation were the panacea for the sufferings of Ireland. The landlords' estates being purchased in the Incumbered Estates' Court as simply and expeditiously as furniture at a sheriff's sale, the mercantile principles had to be applied to the properties purchased by the new capitalist landlords. If capitalists were to invest their money in the purchase of estates, they were entitled to the same freedom of dealing with their lands as was applicable to the case of any other commodity. They claimed and were necessarily allowed, to make the best of their investments by selling what they had bought at the full market value. The obvious right, therefore, of the purchaser was to let his land for the highest rent which a tenant could be induced to offer, because the market value of any article is the highest price which it will fetch at an open competition.

For the purpose of introducing free trade into the relations of landlord and tenant it was necessary to sweep away all lingering tradition of a feudal connection, and to free the parties from the technicalities of an obsolete system of real property.

The framers of the Act of 1860 attempted to simplify the legal relations of landlord and tenant; to consolidate previous statutes; to place the letting of land upon the simple basis of contract; and to modify their rights, in such a manner, and to introduce such new implied agreements as were suitable to the point of view from which they regarded the legal relation in question.

An examination of the important sections of the Act of the 23-24 Vict. ch. 154 shows that it was not drawn in favour of the landlord. The chief provisions of this Act, which regulated the relations of agricultural tenants with their landlords, were as follow :—

I. The relation of landlord and tenant was declared to be one founded on contract, express or implied, and not upon tenure (section 3); by the section the ancient doctrine of the necessity of a reversion was abolished.

II. If a tenant under a written agreement after the expiration of his term continued in possession for one month after a demand for possession by the landlord, such continuance in possession might, at the election of the landlord, be held to create a new tenancy from year to year upon the terms of the previous tenancy (section 5).

III. That in respect of agreements contained or implied in the contract of letting, every assignee of a landlord's interest should have the same right as against the tenant and his assignee as the original landlord had, and that every assignee of a tenant should have the same rights as against the landlord as the original tenant (sections 12 and 13). By these sections a vast amount of legal erudition relative to what contracts did or did not 'run with the land' was swept away, and the assignees of landlord and tenant respectively were considered, not as assignees merely of an estate in the land, but as assignees of the benefit of the original contract.

IV. An assignee of a tenant's interest cannot free himself from the fulfilment of the agreements contained in the original contract by an assignment to a third party without giving notice to the landlord of such assignment, and after the notice continues liable to the payment of the half-yearly gale of rent accruing next after the date of his notice (sections 14 and 15). This was to defeat the common practice of secretly assigning unprofitable leases to paupers.

V. An assignment by a tenant of his interest with the consent in writing of his landlord releases the tenant from future liability under the agreements contained in the original contract (section 16).

VI. The previous law as to fixtures was repealed, and it was enacted that in future 'all personal chattels, engines, machinery, and buildings accessorial thereto, affixed to the freehold by the tenant at his own expense,'—' and so attached to the freehold that they could be removed without substantial injury to the freehold or the fixture itself, and which should not have been erected in pursuance of any obligation or in violation of any agreement, might be removed by the tenant.' This section follows almost the words of the 525th section of the Code Civil, treating of the rules as to accession: 'Le propriétaire est censé avoir attaché à son fonds des effets mobiliers à perpétuelle demeure lorsqu'ils ne peuvent être détachés sans être fracturés et détériorés, ou sans briser ou détériorer la partie du fonds à laquelle ils sont attachés.'

VII. Upon a subletting with the written consent of the landlord, the subtenant by paying his own rent to the tenant is relieved from any liability for the rent, which was reserved by the original lease; but the landlord, if the tenant allows his own rent to run in arrear, can require the subtenant to pay him the rent reserved on the subletting in discharge of the rent reserved by the original lease, and any subtenant may pay off the arrears of the head rent and have credit for such payment as against his own rent (sections 19, 20, and 21).

VIII. In any action brought by a person claiming as an assignee of the original landlord, the fact that the plaintiff, or some person through whom he claims, within three years before the action received the rent for one year, is primâ facie proof of title (section 24).

IX. The tenant of premises containing an open mine may work the mine; any tenant may work open quarries on the lands or cut turf in unreclaimed bog for his own purposes or improvement of the farm, but not for sale (sections 27, 28, 29).

X. A tenant at a rack-rent holding for an uncertain period is entitled to hold, in lieu of emblements, the lands after the determination of his tenancy until 'the last gale day of the current year' (section 34). A tenant at a rent less than the full value retained his common right to emblements.

XI. The destruction of the substantial subject matter of the letting, otherwise than by the default of the tenant, and in the absence of any covenant on the tenant's part to repair, gives to the tenant a right to determine the letting by a surrender (section 40). This section is borrowed from the Civil Law, and repeals the rule of the English Common Law, which, treating the covenants in a lease as collateral to the letting of the land, bound the tenant to pay the covenanted rent during the term, notwithstanding the destruction of the subject matter of the letting.

XII. In every lease (unless it be otherwise expressly agreed) there is to be implied on the part of the landlord covenants for good title to make the lease and for quiet enjoyment by the tenant without interruption by any person, and on the part of the tenant to pay the rent and to give up quiet possession of the premises in good and substantial repair and condition, on the determination of the lease (sections 40 and 41).

XIII. In case of the surrender to, or resumption by, the landlord of any portion of the premises, his rights in respect of the residue of the land shall not be prejudiced (section 44). This section repeals the old rule that in neither of the cases mentioned in the section could the landlord recover any rent out of the residue; such a rule was absurd in the case of a surrender; but under the Civil Law the wrongful resumption by the landlord of any portion of the premises would have suspended his right to recover it.

XIV. In an action for the recovery of rent, the tenant may set off any debts due to him by the landlord (section 48).

XV. A landlord cannot recover by distress more than the rent of the last preceding year (section 51). Previous to 1870 the law considered the feudal process of distress as the primary remedy for the recovery of rent, and the action of ejectment as a secondary or substituted proceeding; thus, in the earlier Acts dealing with ejectments for nonpayment of rent, the right to bring the action was confined to cases in which there was no sufficient distress on the lands. The relation of landlord and tenant being shifted to the basis of contract, the right to distrain could be no longer supported upon its original theory; but if it had been attempted not merely to regulate it but to entirely abolish it, the landlord, not illogically, might have insisted that under a system of contract they were entitled to all the remedies given by the Civil Law for the recovery of rent.

XVI. As to ejectments for the nonpayments of rent, any person substantially and beneficially entitled to the rent may bring an action of ejectment for nonpayment of rent against any tenant, whether holding under a written or *implied* agreement, whenever a year's rent is in arrear; when the year's rent is less than 100*l.* the proceeding may be taken in the County Court; it is sufficient to maintain such an action if a tenancy can be shown to exist between the parties, and all the legal fictions and forms which previously complicated such proceedings are now abolished; the only necessary defendant to such an action is the person in actual possession of the lands as the tenant or subtenant, and the summons (now the writ) is served upon him as in any personal action; if no person is in possession, the summons (now the writ) may be posted on the premises or nearest market town; upon the writ of habere to the sheriff the amount of the rent in arrear and the costs must be endorsed, and the tenant may pay the sheriff up to the moment of execution; at any time within six months after the execution the tenant may pay the amount due for rent and costs *into the court in which the action is brought* and thereupon apply to be restored to possession (sections 51 to 71).

Proceeding upon the same assumption as the Civil Law, that the relation of landlord and tenant was merely a species of hiring, the points in which the Act of 1860 differed from the Civil Law are remarkable; if it did not imply on the part of the landlord that the farm let was a 'possession utile,' or make him in any case participate in the loss arising from a failure of the crop, it neither gave him a hypothec to secure his rent, nor a power to re-enter upon the breach of any agreement of the letting, except upon the nonpayment of the rent; while it treated the relation of landlord and tenant as an ordinary contract, it treated this relation as against both parties, as one *strictissimi juris*, and not to be tempered by the equities so much favoured by the Roman lawyers. The cause of these differences was the different views which the Roman and English lawyers took of the original nature of the contract itself. (1) The former considered a letting of land for a term to be a quasi-sale, with an equitable warranty that the land was worth the annual rent; the latter that it was a mercantile transaction subject to the rule of '*caveat emptor.*' (2) The former considered the rent as the owner's share in the proceeds of the farm, and therefore gave to the landlord the right of hypothec, and compelled him to share in the loss occasioned by a deficient harvest; the latter held the rent as something collateral to the letting—cotemporary but not conditional: the tenant made his bargain, and, as in every other mercantile transaction, ran the chance of gain or loss. (3) The former considered the several agreements of the tenant, whether expressed or implied, as conditions precedent of his possession, and held, therefore, that the landlord could bring his action to re-enter upon the breach of any agreement, expressed or implied; the latter, considering all such agreements (except that for the payment of rent) as collateral, gave the landlord no right to re-enter, and left him to his personal action for damages in all except the one excepted case.

Notwithstanding the differences above referred to, the close resemblance of the Act of 1860 to the French Code is most remarkable; the numerous points of similarity do not appear to have arisen from the study or conscious adoption of the principles of the French system; the form of the sections would lead rather to the conclusion, that its author was wholly ignorant of the Civil or French Law; but these rules are the necessary logical consequence of the assumption common to both systems that the letting of land is to be treated simply as a contract of hiring.

CHAPTER VIII.

THE RESULTS OF THE ACT OF 1860.

THE Act of 1860 swept away every trace of the feudal relation between landlord and tenant; the landlord, certainly, since the passing of this Act, has no more right to claim from his tenants any personal respect or political obedience than the shopkeeper from his customers; the tenant has no more claim for the assistance and sympathy of the landlord than he has for that of his grocer. They occupy in respect of each other simply the relation of any other merchant and his customers. If free trade in land was to be desired, it was facilitated by this Act; if the simplification of the law was advantageous, this Act largely promoted it. Henceforth, the landlord was to differ from the village baker, butcher, grocer, or publican, merely in the nature of the article in which he traded. Feudal duties perish with feudal rights: the owner of land lets it to the tenant, and the tenant hires the land from the landlord; the transaction does not differ—and it was intended that it should not differ—from the chartering of a ship or the hiring of a street cab: the hirers of land henceforth owe no special respect, and need show no deference to their landlord: if the tenants pay the rent which they have agreed to pay, and perform their agreements of the letting, they are as independent of the landlord as of the village huckster—when they have settled their pass-book; but, if so, what claim have they longer on their landlord for protection, assistance, or forbearance? Why should he, more than any other, be expected to aid the poor, assist in local charities, give a site for the parish chapel, or be considerate in the collection of his debts?

By free trade in land Ireland was to be regenerated, and those who were to take the benefit of the system were bound to accept its drawbacks.

The objection to the application of a land law founded upon contract to the relations of landlords and tenants in Ireland lay, not in the injustice of the law itself nor in any advantage given by it to the landlord as against the tenant (for the system as based on pure contract was strictly just, and the reforms in the law had been made distinctly in favour of the tenant), but in its introduction into a society not adapted for it. As between the landlord and the majority of the tenants, there was not, nor could be, any freedom of contract. The smaller tenants were not possessed of any capital, and lived poorly by their own labour upon their unimproved farms. If deprived of their farms they had no other means of livelihood; the demand for land so far exceeded the supply that they had no hopes of establishing themselves elsewhere, and therefore the interest of a tenant in a farm fetched a price absurdly large as compared with the returns to be had from the land. A tenant once turned out of his holding had no means of existence; to him and his family the loss of his tenancy meant starvation and death. When served with a notice to quit the farmer was willing to offer any rent for a new letting of his holding, regardless of his ability to pay it in subsequent years. From the very nature of the tenancy from year to year many tenants naturally regarded their farms as their own property, subject to the payment of the usual rent. Upon farms held under this tenure families had lived for generations; the land had been in many cases reclaimed and improved by themselves or their fathers; and when it had not been so they believed that it had; easy-going and unenterprising they never realised the possibility of a notice to quit, and when it was served upon them it seemed an act of unjust oppression and a sudden destruction.

The energetic purchaser in the Landed Estates Court generally served notices to quit upon all the yearly tenants with a view to a 'readjustment of the rents,' and having thus increased his income, either congratulated himself upon the large returns upon his investment, or sold to another capitalist his estate enhanced in value by a fictitious rental.

It is but just to state that in the vast majority of estates the relations between landlord and tenant continued unchanged, and in many instances where rents were increased the increase of the rent was warranted by the increased price of farming produce.

Most of the ejectments also were not for the purpose of increasing the rent; many were brought with the object of substituting large for small farms; many were brought for the purpose of stripping the land and improving the holdings of the tenants themselves; and many were rendered necessary by the quarrels of the members of the family of a deceased tenant contending for the succession to the farm. But it must be remembered, in justice to the tenants, that every notice to quit brought home to the tenant the power of the landlord to evict him; every use by a landlord of his legal power for the purpose of raising the rent or obtaining a fine from some incoming tenant was a conclusive proof that this power might be harshly and inequitably used; even when an estate was justly and humanely managed, the tenants were well aware that their landlord might die, and that upon his death his property might be sold by the Landed Estates Court, in small lots, to country shopkeepers or local capitalists—the most greedy of purchasers and worst of landlords.

The principle of free trade in land had failed to improve the condition of Ireland; the statutory declaration of this doctrine had terrified the tenants into increasing agitation, and it became necessary either not to enforce the new theory of law until the population were so improved as to be capable of appreciating an advanced Code (an event certainly not likely soon to occur), or to introduce legislation of an admittedly retrograde character, for the purpose of palliating patent evils and allaying not ill-founded discontent.

CHAPTER IX.

THE IRISH LAND ACT OF 1870.

The Landlord and Tenant Act, 1870 (33 and 34 Vict. ch. 46), better known as the Irish Land Act, sought, according to those who were responsible for it, to accomplish three principal objects:

1. To obtain for the tenants in Ireland 'security of tenure.' 2. To encourage the making of improvements throughout the country; and, 3, to create a peasant proprietorship in Ireland. The Act itself is divided into five parts. The first part deals with the occupation of land. The second part deals with its ownership, and endeavours to facilitate the purchase of their holdings by tenants from their landlords. The third part enables the Board of Public Works in Ireland to advance money for the purposes of the Act. The fourth and fifth parts contain some miscellaneous clauses and definitions in connection with this Act. Reference is here made only to those sections which materially affected the relation of landlords and tenants.

The Act made no alterations in the tenancies held under the Ulster Tenant Right Custom; it merely gave legal sanction to, and enforced, the

Ulster Custom against the landlords of the estates which were subject to it. The tenants of these estates were secured the benefit of the custom, but not bound to hold under it, for any such tenant could abandon his right under the custom, and claim the rights given to all tenants by the statute.

What course should be adopted in obtaining for tenants, whose rights were to be regulated by the Act of 1870, 'Security of tenure,' was a matter of the utmost difficulty. It was not possible in 1870 to state openly that free trade in land was the real cause of the renewed agitation of the Irish tenantry, or to propose that the rights of those who had invested their capital under a State guarantee in the purchase of lands in the Landed Estates Court should be diminished, without compensation, for the public benefit.

The law of Great Britain and Ireland had persistently refused to recognise any interest or co-proprietorship in the occupier of the soil apart from a mere permission to cultivate it. The land itself was the absolute property of the landlord, subject to the existing contracts under which it had been hired out to the tenants. The purchaser in the Landed Estates Court had purchased this absolute ownership in the land, subject only to the existing tenancies. By his purchase he was guaranteed the property in, and actual possession of, the land upon the termination of the tenancies in the schedule, and the protection of the law in the exercise of his legal right of determining the existing yearly tenancies. The right of forcing the yearly tenants to pay the full market value of their farms, or of clearing them off the land, was notoriously put forward as an inducement to such purchasers.

The framers of the Act dared not to state openly (and it was constantly denied) that the object of this statute was to give the tenant any estate in the land, or to transfer to him any portion of the absolute ownership. The Act, therefore, apparently gave the tenant no new rights, nor in anywise deprived the landlord of any; but attempted to effect its object in a circuitous manner by affixing what was essentially a penalty to the exercise of rights which it admitted to be legal. The Act in fact said to the landlords, 'Your right to evict your tenants is incontestable, no one could dream of depriving you of what is most certainly your property; you may, of course, turn out your tenants as you like, but it shall be made so expensive a proceeding that you will think seriously before you attempt it.' This was described as a process by which bad landlords were obliged to act as the good landlords did; it might be more justly stated to be an enactment by which the amusement of evicting tenants was made a monopoly of the wealthier proprietors.

Thus the rights given to the tenants as against their landlords are not stated affirmatively in the statute; the rights of the tenant are, so to say, latent, and cannot be exercised until the landlord has previously attempted to exercise his legal right of resuming the possession. Until the landlord 'disturbed' the tenant, the rights of the latter were precisely the same as they were before the Act; from the date of the disturbance, the tenant acquired a negative right of refusing to give up the possession without compensation. Under this statute the tenant did not acquire any 'estate' in the land, if the term 'estate' is used in its technical English meaning; but of the ownership of the land, whether the word be used in its popular or proper meaning, he did acquire a share; for if a man cannot be put out of possession by the rightful owner without the payment of a certain sum of money, he is an owner to the extent of the sum requisite to buy him out.

The Act of 1870 is not intended to regulate the relations and rights of all landlords and tenants, for it does not apply to any holding which is not agricultural or pastoral in its character, and therefore excludes all lettings of houses and of lands which, although more or less tilled or grazed, are taken for residential and not farming purposes (section 71). The Act also excludes from its operation the letting of demesne lands and town parks, holdings by servants or hired labourers, lettings for purposes of temporary grazing, and lettings acknowledged in writing to be made for the purpose of temporary convenience.

Tenants entitled to the benefit of the Ulster Custom must elect whether they will claim under the custom or the general provisions; they cannot of course obtain the advantages of both species of tenure.

The leading provisions of the Act are as follows:—

It introduces an entirely new rule of law as to what is styled compensation for disturbance. Any tenant of any holding under a tenancy created after the passing of the Act (less than a lease for thirty-one years [1]) if disturbed in his holding by the act of the landlord, and any tenant from year to year of any holding rated at not more than

---

[1] The extent to which the right of free contract in land was affected by this section is not at first perceived. If A now let by lease to B an agricultural holding in Ireland for the term of thirty years, the 42nd section of the Act of 1860, which is still law, declares that there shall be implied in this lease a covenant on the part of the tenant to give peaceable possession of the demised premises on the determination of the lease; but the Act of 1870 interposes, and forbids the landlord to require of the tenant the fulfilment of this covenant without paying him *compensation* for so doing. The object of the Act of 1870 was to render it the interest of the landlord to grant leases for thirty-one years by making it expensive for him to get up the land from tenants holding for a shorter term or lesser interest, but the selection of the phrase 'compensation for *disturbance*' was most unfortunate. It may be conjectured that it was suggested by the case of tenancies from year to year determined by a notice to quit, but how a tenant for a fixed term of years could be described as '*disturbed* by his landlord,' upon the regular effluxion of the term for which he had taken the lands, it is difficult to understand.

100*l.* per annum, if disturbed by the act of his *immediate* landlord, is entitled to such compensation for the loss which the Court shall find to be sustained by him by reason of quitting his holding as the Court shall think fit.

The maximum of the compensation is fixed as follows:—

- *a.* (1) If the tenancy be valued on the Government valuation at 10*l.*, or under, per annum, seven years' rent.
  - (2) If valued at or under 30*l.* per annum, five years' rent.
  - (3) If valued at or under 40*l.* per annum, four years' rent.
  - (4) If valued at or under 50*l.* per annum, three years' rent.
  - (5) If valued at or under 100*l.* per annum, two years' rent.
  - (6) If valued above 100*l.* per annum, one year's rent.
- *b.* The compensation is in no case to exceed 250*l.*
- *c.* No tenant of a holding valued above 10*l.* per annum, and claiming more than four years' rent, and no tenant of a holding valued at less than 10*l.* per annum, and claiming more than five years' rent, shall be entitled to an additional claim for improvements other than permanent buildings and reclamation of waste land.

Out of such compensation a deduction is to be made for—(1) arrears of rent; (2) damages for the deterioration of the holding arising from the non-observance of any expressed or implied covenants or agreements.

Any tenant who sublets or divides his holding without written permission, or who, in despite of a written prohibition, lets any part in conacre, is disentitled to compensation for disturbance.

A tenant holding under a lease for not less than thirty-one years is not entitled to compensation for disturbance.

The scale of compensation for disturbance adopted in this Act is not based upon the value of the tenant's interest in the land; it is quite inconsistent with such a supposition that a maximum amount of compensation should be fixed, or that the tenant of a holding rated at ten pounds should receive seven times as many years' purchase as the tenant of a holding rated over a hundred.

It must be further observed that, inasmuch as the maximum of the compensation in each case is calculated upon the basis, not of the valuation, but of the rent, the amount of compensation varies in the inverse ratio of the value of the interest, which has been lost by the tenant. The higher the rent reserved upon a lease, the less will it fetch at an auction; and on the other hand its value would be augmented if the rent were reduced. If A be tenant from year to year of a farm valued at 10*l*., and pays a rent of 15*l*. per annum, and B holds a farm of equal rating but pays only 5*l*. per annum rent, it is manifest that B's interest in his holding is much more valuable than that of A.; under this section, however, A would be entitled to the sum of 105*l*. as compensation for disturbance, but B only to 35*l*.

The absurdity of compensating a tenant in the direct, and not in the inverse ratio of his rent is not peculiar to this Act, but occurs in other well-known schemes devised for the benefit of the Irish tenantry.

It may be asked if the compensation has no connection with the money-value of the tenant's interest, for what is the compensation given? Apparently for the inconvenience caused to the tenant by breaking up his home and seeking for another farm. But by what standard is the damage for such personal inconvenience to be measured? The actual inconvenience and loss must depend upon many circumstances connected with the tenant's family and mode of life, the number, age, and health of his family, the existence of some other business or employment of the tenant unconnected with his holding, the probability of his obtaining a similar farm in the neighbourhood—but it does seem very illogical that the amount of compensation, to be paid by the disturbing landlord, should depend upon the number of the family and mode of life of the disturbed tenant. Left thus without any clue as to the principles upon which the amount of compensation should be assessed, the County Court Judges have taken the maximum fixed by the Act as the amount to which any tenant is *primâ facie* entitled, leaving it to the landlord to reduce it by bringing forward proof of unreasonable conduct on the part of the tenant. The unlimited and indefinite jurisdiction given to the County Court Judges paralysed their action, and they naturally evaded the performance of an impossible duty by the establishment of an absurd and inflexible rule, which gave the maximum of compensation alike to the cottier whose household was broken up and his livelihood imperilled, and to the grazier who had taken a grazing-farm without house or homestead upon it.

The rule which fixes the class of a holding by reference to its rating, and the amount of compensation by reference to the rent, renders it dangerous for a landlord to improve lands in his hands with the view of letting them subsequently to tenants. The mode in which this occurs may be more easily understood by stating the facts of an existing case: P. R—— is possessed of a residence and demesne, adjoining to which, at the date of the Poor Law valuation, was an extensive and unprofitable marsh; this tract was, and remains, rated for Poor Law and fiscal purposes at 6*d.* per acre; P. R—— has lately drained and improved this land, and rendered it so valuable that he is offered by tenants

1*l.* 16*s.* 0*d.* per acre for portions of it, but the state of the law and the merest prudence must prevent him letting it for a less term than 31 years, and the position of the land in connection with his demesne naturally renders him unwilling to do so. If he let 100 acres of this land to a tenant from year to year, the legal condition of affairs would be as follows: the 100 acres being valued at only 6*d.* per acre, the rated value of the entire holding would be 2*l.* 10*s.* 0*d.*, and the holding therefore would fall within the first class, and the tenant if disturbed be entitled to seven years' rent as compensation; in consequence of the landlord's improvements in this case the rent to be paid by the tenant would be 180*l.*, and therefore the amount to be paid to the tenant if disturbed would be 1260*l.*, and any agreement between the landlord and tenant to avoid this result would be absolutely void at law. In this case, if the owner were foolish enough to let the lands, his improvements would be clearly confiscated for the benefit of the tenant, and, inasmuch as land, as distinguished from buildings, cannot be revalued, under the Irish Valuation Act, the difficulty thus created cannot be removed by re-valuation.

A landlord rarely disturbed a farmer who paid his rent, unless there were some other tenant ready to take the farm at an increased rent, and the unpleasantness attending an eviction, if no better motive, rendered landlords unwilling to enter into such transactions unless this increase was very considerable. The scale of compensation for disturbance unfortunately rendered the landlords willing to accede to the application of any tenant who desired to obtain his neighbour's farm and offered an indemnity against the compensation and costs. The following imaginary case may explain why the Act produced this unexpected result. If a landlord have four tenants, A, B, C, and D (of whom A, B, and C hold farms valued at 10l. each, and subject respectively to 12l. rent, and D holds a farm valued at 71l. at a rent of 90l.), and himself *disturb* these four tenants, he must pay the following compensation —84l. to each of A, B, and C, and 180l. to D., in all 432l. D being a wealthy man proposes to the landlord that he will pay the compensation and costs incident to the disturbance of A B and C, if their holdings are re-let to him and thrown into his farm; in such a transaction, D would probably offer an increase of rent, but even without this additional inducement it is the landlord's interest to accept the offer, for A, B, and C, having been ejected, their holdings are thrown into D's farm, who thereupon holds a farm valued at 101l. per annum, and subject to the yearly rent of 126l., and the landlord can, if he subsequently desire it, consequently obtain possession of the whole at the moderate compensation to D of 126l.

The compensation for disturbance being damages payable by the landlord, who, for his own purposes, puts an end to the tenancy (?), if the act of the landlord be the consequence of the tenant's own breach of the terms of his agreement, it cannot be considered as disturbance of the tenant's interest. A tenant, therefore, ejected for nonpayment of rent, or for the breach of a covenant against assignment, or subletting, or on bankruptcy or insolvency, is treated as if he himself were the cause of the action of the landlord, and is placed in the same position as if he had himself voluntarily surrendered his holding; that is, he is entitled to compensation for improvements, but not for disturbance.

It was essential to the working of the scheme embodied in the Act that a tenant from year to year, evicted for nonpayment of rent or breach of covenant should not be entitled to compensation for disturbance; if it made no difference in the tenant's right to compensation for disturbance, whether he were evicted by an ejectment founded upon a notice to quit or for nonpayment of rent, it must follow that the nonpayment of rent was not unreasonable conduct on the part of the tenant, in respect of which the Judge should declare the tenant not entitled to the full compensation for disturbance; if the law were so, it would be possible for a landlord to be compelled to make considerable payments to his tenants, and yet never himself to receive any rent from them; *e.g.*, if A lets to B, as tenant from year to year, a farm valued at 9*l*. per annum, and subject to a rent of 12*l*. per annum, and B never pays any rent to A, who, after the expiration of the first year of the tenancy, brings his ejectment for non-payment of rent against B, B would be entitled to 84*l*. for disturbance, against which A could set off 12*l*. for one year's rent, and thus B, having enjoyed the farm gratis for one year, would yet receive 72*l*. as consideration for his departure.

To the rule that an ejectment for nonpayment of rent does not constitute a disturbance, there are introduced two remarkable exceptions: (1) If in the case of a tenancy existing at the passing of the Act more than three years of rent have been allowed by the landlord to fall into arrear; and (2) in the case of tenancies not exceeding 15*l*. if the Court should be of opinion that the rent is exorbitant (section 9).[1]

[1] The logical process upon which this enactment is based would seem to be as follows: A lets land to B as tenant from year to year at the rent of 12*l*. per annum. If A serves a notice to quit and brings an ejectment on the title, he disturbs B. If B does not pay the rent, and A brings an ejectment for nonpayment of rent, B has caused A to disturb him. If A has *induced* B to agree to pay a rent, which in fact he can not, having reference to the value of the lands, A has caused B to be unable to pay the rent, the nonpayment of which is the grounds for A bringing his ejectment. But if B induces A to put him into possession of the lands by voluntarily *offering* too high a rent, is not B himself the ultimate cause of the disturbance? The framer had in his mind the case of a poor tenant whose rent had been forced up by the landlord, not that of a reckless competitor for the possession of lands, who of his own accord offered to the landlord what was in fact an exorbitant rent.

A landlord cannot be required to accept an assignee of a tenant if such assignee be of objectionable character, or if he be forced upon the landlord under unreasonable circumstances; therefore a landlord is not considered guilty of disturbance if he eject—(1) the assignee of a tenant who is himself liable to ejectment for non-payment of rent; (2) or whom he has not consented to accept as his tenant, when it is the custom of his estate to ask such consent; or (3) to whom personally, in the opinion of the Court, he had reasonable cause of objection (section 13).

Subject to the maximum fixed, the amount of compensation for disturbance is left to the County Court Judge, who has the fullest discretion to take all the surrounding circumstances into consideration and to regard the conduct of the tenant himself. In certain cases of wanton and unreasonable acts by the tenant, the Act deprives him of all right of compensation (section 14), and the principle laid down in this section is subsequently made applicable in fixing the amount of compensation to be given (section 18). As a general rule the courts allow the tenant the maximum fixed by the Act, unless there be reasonable cause to reduce this amount.

The Act next proceeds to deal with the question of compensation for 'improvements,' which are defined to mean works which, being executed, add to the letting value of the holding, and are suitable thereto, the benefit of which is unexhausted at the time of the tenant's quitting the holding.¹

The rules as to such claims for compensation are as follows:—

Any tenant on quitting his holding may claim compensation in respect of all improvements on his holding, made by himself or his predecessors in title, subject to the following exceptions:—

    1. Improvements made twenty years before the claim, other than permanent buildings, and the reclamation of waste land.
    2. Improvements prohibited by the landlord, in writing, as diminishing the general value of his property, and considered by the Court to be of such a nature.
    3. Improvements executed in pursuance of a contract.
    4. Improvements made in contravention of a contract in writing.
    5. Improvements made which the landlord had undertaken to make.
    6. Improvements compensation for which is expressly excluded by the terms of a lease made before the Act.
    7. A tenant under a lease for thirty-one

---

¹ This definition, as restricted by the rules, is almost the same as the sentence in the Digest, 'In conducto fundo, si conductor suâ operâ aliquid necessario vel utiliter auxerit, vel ædificaverit, vel instituerit, cum id non convenisset ad recipienda quæ impendit,' &c. *D.*, *l.* 19, 2, 55, 1.

years certain, or a lease which has in fact subsisted for thirty-one years, can claim compensation only for permanent buildings and the reclamation of waste land.

8. A tenant is not entitled to compensation for improvements if his landlord has given him permission to dispose of his claim for improvements to the incoming tenant, upon reasonable terms, and he has refused or neglected to do so.

9. In calculating the amount of compensation to be made for improvements, the time during which the tenant himself has had the benefit of it is to be taken into account.

Any tenant whose holdings, or aggregate holdings, in Ireland are valued under the Government valuation at not less than 50*l.* per annum, may contract himself out of the provisions of the Act as to compensation for disturbance or improvements; in the case of tenants whose holdings are of a less value, such a contract is void (sections 4 & 12).

The tenant can hold possession of his farm until the amount of compensation has been paid by the landlord.

The tenant during the currency of the letting is enabled to preserve the evidence of the fact that improvements have been made, by filing a schedule of the improvements so made in the

Landed Estates Court, according to the course of practice prescribed by the Judges' rules on the subject.

To prevent the objects of the Act being defeated by the creation of tenancies at will, &c., it is provided that a letting of land for a tenancy at will, or any tenancy less than a tenancy from year to year, creates, notwithstanding the terms of the agreement, a tenancy from year to year (section 69).[1]

The provisions of the Act as to disturbance being framed upon the assumption that the landlord by some act of his terminates the holding of his own tenant, it is clear that the case of sub-tenants was overlooked by the drafter of the sections 3 and 4. If lands were let in 1775 to a tenant for the term of 100 years, and the tenant or his representatives sublet the lands to numerous small yearly tenants at an increased rent, and under these circumstances the term of 100 years determines in 1875, what are the rights of the subtenants? The representative of the original lessor is entitled to the possession of the lands demised upon the termination of the lease; he certainly cannot take up the lands with the tenants upon it, for if by any act he created an implied tenancy between himself and the sub

---

[1] The result of this section is that if A lets land to B for six months, from the 1st of January 1880, he cannot recover the possession until the 1st of July 1881, and will then have to pay to B compensation for 'disturbing' him.

tenants, he could not remove them without the payment of compensation for disturbance. To clear the land he is forced by the provisions of the Act itself. Against whom can the subtenants when ejected claim compensation? Certainly not against the head landlord, who never was their immediate landlord nor let them the lands, and who is clearly entitled, as against his tenant and all claiming under him, to get back his lands in the state in which he let them; nor against the middleman, who is himself disturbed. The subtenant's interest in the lands cannot last longer than that of his immediate landlord, and all the subtenancies must fall with the middle interest. Evidently to remedy this oversight the 20th section was introduced into a portion of the Act quite foreign to its subject. The result of this section may be stated thus: The tenant whose interest has determined for the purpose of the Act is the middleman, and he may be entitled to some compensation for disturbance or otherwise as against the head landlord. What the landlord is bound to pay is determined by the position of his immediate tenant; this is all the money available for the compensation of the occupying tenants, and this amount being secured for the benefit of the subtenants, the Court directs the payment thereof by such person and to one or more of the parties interested and in such manner as it thinks just. The practical working of this section is as follows:—
If A let 99 acres, valued at 99l. per annum, to

eleven tenants from year to year in equal proportions at the rent of 12*l.* per annum each, he must pay them 84*l.* each (924*l.* among all) for the purpose of regaining possession of his land; on the other hand if A let 101 acres valued at 101*l.* per annum to B as tenant from year to year, at the annual rent of 132*l.*, being the same as he received in the former case, and B makes eleven lettings thereout similar to the former, and A serves notice to quit, the entire sum divisible among B and all his under-tenants is only the sum of 132*l.*; the loss by disturbance to the under-tenants is the same in one case as the other, but the compensation in the former is seven times that in the latter.

The Act further attempted to benefit the tenants by giving to every tenant for a term certain, as well as for an uncertain period, the right to remove his away-going crops, or the value thereof (section 8), and it also threw one-half of the county cess upon the landlord (section 65). What justification there was for this rule in the case of existing contracts it is not easy to perceive, but as to future contracts it could merely produce an alteration in the rent or a special covenant. As it was the object of the Act to compel landlords to grant agricultural leases for terms of at least thirty-one years, it was necessary also to empower tenants for life, &c., to make leases of this duration, so as to bind thereby the persons entitled in remainder. Limited owners (as de-

THE IRISH LAND ACT OF 1870. 81

fined by the 28th section) were therefore enabled by the 28th section to grant such leases for terms not exceeding thirty-five years, subject, of course, to the usual conditions annexed in marriage settlements to the exercise of a leasing power. From no cause had improving tenants suffered more severely than from leases granted by limited owners being set aside as being outside the leasing power. Harsh as the decisions of the Courts in many such cases may seem, the ordinary experience of life teaches that if leases, &c., made by a tenant for life in excess or in violation of his power were not at once set aside, there would be not much left for the remainder man to succeed to, and that those whose sufferings are the most descanted upon are often actively, more often negligently, themselves parties to the fraud committed. To remedy this evil, a lease executed under the leasing power contained in the 28th section may be brought by either the limited owner or the tenant before the County Court Judge, who inquires into the transaction, and whose confirmation thereof, in the manner subsequently prescribed by the Judges' rules, is conclusive evidence of the lease being within the powers given by the Act.

It was attempted by the clauses of the Act 32–41, commonly known as the Bright Clauses, to carry out the third object which the framers of the Act had in view—the creation of a peasant proprietary in Ireland.

The scheme embodied in these clauses was that a landlord (whether an absolute owner, tenant for life, or limited owner, as defined by the Act) might come to an agreement with a tenant for the sale to such tenant of the fee simple of the holding of the tenant; that an application should be made on behalf of the contracting parties to the Landed Estates Court to approve of and carry out the sale by a Landed Estates Court conveyance to the tenant; that the purchase money should be lodged in court, and represent for all purposes the estate conveyed to the tenants; and the holding, free from incumbrances, should be vested in the tenant in fee, or, in case of the landlord's tenure being leasehold, for the term of such lease, and subject to the rent and covenants thereof.

The total failure of these sections to effect their proposed object, even when both landlord and tenant were anxious to carry out their agreement, has often been a subject of wonder, but the cause of their failure is obvious to any who are acquainted with the nature of the Landed Estates Court title, which it was considered desirable for the tenant to obtain. A Landed Estates Court conveyance affects not only the rights of the parties to the proceedings, but binds all persons, whether parties or not, and extinguishes all rights which are inconsistent with the terms of the grant by the Court. If, by any mistake, more lands than should properly be sold are included in the grant, or the most indisputable rights of third parties are not noticed in the body of the grant or the annexed schedule, irreparable injustice is done, and the injured parties have no redress. This absolute and drastic effect of a Landed Estates Court conveyance was the leading principle adopted at the establishment of the Incumbered Estates Court, and is the basis upon which rests the security and value of the conveyances made by these Courts. It is obvious that the exercise of such a jurisdiction requires the utmost attention on the part of the Judge, and the fact that the Court was not made the instrument for the perpetuation of the grossest frauds is due solely to the stringency of its rules and the intelligence of its officers.

An additional element of difficulty necessarily arose when the Court was required to act under these clauses for the purpose of carrying into effect a contract entered into between a limited owner and tenant, for it was possible, and in many cases not improbable, that the transaction involved a fraud to be effected as against parties entitled in remainder or incumbrancers; the price might be wholly inadequate, and the tenant for life receive a douceur as the consideration for his entering into such an arrangement. The Court was required by the Act itself to inquire into the circumstances of the holding; the parties interested, other than the parties to the contract; and the sufficiency of the price (section 34). This preliminary inquiry involved considerable expense, both of statements to be lodged for the information of the Court and notices to the parties interested; many of whom would probably be found to be either absent from the country, minors, or married women. When this merely preliminary inquiry was concluded the case had to be proceeded with as in the ordinary course of a sale. The Court had to inquire what interest in the land the contracting landlord represented: he might be only a tenant in fee farm, and the mines, &c., belong to a third party; or he might himself be a lessee for a term of years, or under a lease for lives renewable or not; the title of the owner must therefore be gone into to prevent frauds upon a second class of persons. It was also necessary to inquire as to the title of the tenant who desired to purchase the interest of his landlord, as he might have only a limited interest in the estate of the lessee, or hold it subject to incumbrances; or, indeed, although paying the rent, might have no title at all thereto, and be desirous, by obtaining an absolute conveyance from the Landed Estates Court, of effecting a fraud as against those truly entitled. Thus the interest of a third class of persons had to be protected. Further, even when these inquiries are exhausted, the rights of adjoining owners and of the public must be considered; the lands to be sold must be surveyed, copies of the maps served upon the adjoining owners, and advertisements published to protect public rights of way, &c. Such a procedure is necessary if the conveyance is to be absolute, and the costs of all such inquiries bear no relation to the value of the estate; they are comparatively insignificant in the case of a large, but relatively great in that of a small estate. In the case of the necessary sale of an incumbered estate the costs are, as a rule, the first charge upon the proceeds of the sale,[1] but when the Court is asked to carry out an agreement under these clauses the costs, except those of the distribution of the purchase money, must be provided for by the parties themselves, that is, practically be paid by the tenant, who, to provide for the expense of serving notices, preparing maps, &c., must therefore initiate the proceeding by depositing in Court 'such sum as the Court may require' (section 34). If the tenant be willing to incur the expenses necessarily incident to the purchase of the fee, a further difficulty remains to the completion of the transaction, which seriously affects the value of the estate to be thereby acquired.

It is true that the estate conveyed to the

[1] By the 78th section of the Landed Estates Court Act the costs of an incumbrancer are payable out of the proceeds in the same priority as his incumbrance; but as this section contained the words 'unless the judge shall otherwise direct,' the rule intended to have been established thereby has become the exception, indeed has now been declared to be exceptional.—(*In re Hutching*, 11 *Ir. Jur.* N.S. 400.)

tenant will be free from the incumbrances affecting that of the landlord, the rights of the incumbrancers being transferred to the money representing the lands, but under the term 'incumbrances' are not included quit rents, tithe-rent charges, or drainage charges (section 36). Almost all estates in Ireland are subject to charges of this description, the existence of which is immaterial to a tenant paying an annual rent, but most injurious to the purchaser of portion of the estate; for, if an estate subject to such a charge be divided among several purchasers, the owner of the rent need not embarrass himself by proceeding against them all collectively (a course which would involve much difficulty and expense), but may require the owner of any portion of the land to pay the entire rent-charge, and in his turn to proceed against his co-owners for contribution. To obviate this difficulty the Act gave the Court power to apportion rent-charges and covenants by a section (No. 40) which was intended to be similar to the 72nd section of the Landed Estates Court Act, which gave the Court power to apportion head-rents in the case of a fee simple estate, but required notice to be given of such intended apportionment to the owner of the rent, who was manifestly entitled to be heard in relation to the matter. The Court has always been slow and unwilling to exercise the power of apportioning rent-charges upon the premises sold, and requires it to be clearly shown that the interest of the rent should not in any appreciable degree be made less secure, or less enjoyable, or less marketable. It is idle to suppose that the property of the owner of the head-rent would not be seriously depreciated by being broken into several smaller rent-charges apportioned among the holdings of the tenants who had purchased the fee under the sections in question. A rent-charge of 100*l*. per annum charged upon a large estate is a first-class security, and fetches a high price in the market; but fifty annuities of 2*l*. each charged upon separate portions of the estate would be difficult to collect and impossible to sell. The Court has, therefore, refused to exercise its power to apportion such charges, except in very exceptional cases. However advantageous it may be to create a peasant proprietary, it has been held that the process should not be carried out to the injury of third parties. The usual mode adopted in the sale of estates subject to such charges is to set aside some one lot of considerable value, and to sell it primarily subject to the rent-charge which affects all the lots sold, and to declare the other lots entitled to be indemnified thereout against the payment of the rent-charge. By this practice the rights of the owner of the rent-charge are unaffected; and, inasmuch as the primary liability of the selected lot is stated in all the conveyances, the purchasers of the indemnified lots have a complete security. Unfortunately a tenant purchasing under these clauses cannot ask the Court to adopt this course, because if the payment of the entire rent-charge be thrown upon the residue of the landlord's estate in indemnification of the holding of the tenant who first applies under these clauses, the result must be to render similar applications by the remaining tenants to purchase their holdings more and more difficult, and ultimately impossible.

A more practical system for the creation of a tenant proprietary is contained in the 44th section, which enables the Board of Public Works in Ireland, when an estate is sold in the Landed Estates Court, to advance to any tenant, who purchases his holding, any sum not exceeding two-thirds of the purchase money, to be repaid by an annuity after the rate of 5*l.* per cent., per annum, for thirty-five years. Many tenants have complained that the Board have failed to carry out the spirit of this section; but in most of the cases in which such complaints have been made, they in fact amount to an objection to the rules as to such advances adopted by the Board, which, although recognising the benefit of a peasant proprietary, could not forget that they were trustees of public money, and insisted upon unquestionable security for the advances which they were requested to make.

It is further provided by this Act that the Landed Estates Court, on the sale of an estate, shall, *as far as is consistent with the interests of the persons interested in the estate or the purchase money,* afford by the formation of lots, or otherwise, all reasonable facilities to occupying tenants desirous of purchasing their holdings (section 46).

This well-meaning but loosely drawn section has been the cause of many disputes and much litigation, culminating in the celebrated case of ' In re Pemberton, Trustee of Harenc.' The ultimate result of the decisions seems to be that occupying tenants, whatever be their position or circumstances, have a primâ-facie right to have the estate for sale divided into lots co-extensive with their holdings. They have also a right to be *otherwise* facilitated by the Judge in purchasing their holdings. But their right is restricted whenever the subdivision of the estate, or any other facility claimed by the tenants, appears to the Judge inconsistent with the interests of the parties interested in the estate or the purchase money.

The leading alterations introduced by this Act into the relation of landlord and tenant are those contained in the 3rd and 4th sections, which regulate the compensations payable to tenants upon the occasion of a disturbance or in respect of improvements.

As regards the smaller tenancies from year to year, existing at the date of the Act itself, and all tenancies of that class created subsequently, the principle of compensation for disturbance is founded on substantial justice, although somewhat shocking to the preconceived ideas of English lawyers. It is true that when the tenant took the farm as a yearly tenant he was aware of the incidents of such tenure, and that upon service of a notice to quit the tenancy was terminated by an Act which the tenant should have taken into his calculations, and by the exercise of a right which the landlord expressly reserved to himself; but, in truth, the moral relation and understanding between a landlord and such a tenant varies from the strictly legal one. No landlord could let the holding, nor could a tenant be found to take it, were there not a tacit understanding that the landlord would not arbitrarily exercise his rights, and that unless some extraordinary and unforeseen event occurred, he would allow the tenant to remain in possession so long as he paid the stipulated, or a fairly increased, rent. If the claim of the tenant not to be wantonly disturbed had no legal grounds to support it, perhaps it had some equitable, certainly it had moral. As to the amount of compensation to be paid on account of such an equity, the Act affords no measure or standard, except that certain limits are laid down, not to be exceeded, in the tenant's favour. The difficulty of stating the principle upon which these damages should be assessed was thus awkwardly eluded, and the entire question was thrown upon the County Court Judge, who was left as best he might to settle the disputes between the parties.

Conceding the equitable or moral grounds upon which a tenant from year to year might be admitted to claim compensation for disturbance, it is difficult to see upon what theory tenants for terms certain exceeding a tenancy from year to year should also be allowed compensation for disturbance upon the termination of the letting.

The object of the rule is plainly to make it the interest of the landlords to grant leases for the full term of thirty-one years; but as in a letting for a fixed period the maximum amount to be paid for disturbance at the termination of the interest is known, and the date of the payment certain, the annual rent will be fixed with reference to it in a manner rather to the disadvantage of the tenant, for the landlord must for his own security increase the rent so as to insure against the maximum of compensation.

In considering the right of a tenant to compensation for improvements it is necessary clearly to keep in view the definition of improvements contained in the Act. A tenant may spend large sums of money upon his holding without entitling himself to any compensation : his right depends, not upon the fact of the expenditure of money, but upon the result of the expenditure. An eccentric tenant of an agricultural farm may build thereon a villa residence, a kennel for hounds, a stable for a racing stud, or a tower commanding an extensive prospect, or he may lay it out in flower beds, or shrubberies ; but such works, although requiring a large expenditure, would not add to *the value of the holding as an agricultural farm;* and if the landlord were required to repay the tenant such expenditure, the tenant would either succeed 'in improving the landlord out of his estate,' or the landlord would be required to indemnify the tenant against the consequences of his own extravagance. The landlord's liability to pay rests upon the principle 'qui ne permet pas de s'enrichir aux dépens d'autrui.' In so far as the property at the termination of the letting is worth more for the purposes of its ordinary occupation by reason of the expenditure of the tenant's money, such increased value represents the tenant's money, and to the extent of the increase of value he is entitled to security for his expenditure. Even if the increase of value arise incidentally from the application of the tenant's capital, he has been held entitled to compensation. Thus when a tenant was in the habit of purchasing from neighbouring farmers large quantities of green crops with which his cattle were outfed, and it was proved that this treatment had largely increased the value and improved the fertility of land, the Judge held that the tenant was entitled to compensation, not under the head of unexhausted manures, but for improvements which added to the letting value of the holding.

By the Act of 1860 the tenant was secured all the rights which arise under a system of free contract; the Act of 1870 leaves untouched all the advantages given to the tenant by the preceding statute, and secures him in a negative form further valuable rights independent of, and often in direct contradiction to, the contract under which he entered into possession. He cannot be put out of his holding without compensation. When he quits, even of his own free will, or even when ejected for nonpayment of his rent, he is entitled to compensation for all improvements. Special facilities are given him if he desire to purchase the landlord's interest, and if he has not sufficient money for the purpose he can obtain an advance from Government.

The authors of the measure may justly have imagined that they had gained for the Irish tenants security of tenure, and yet now ten years after the Act was passed the complaints of the tenants are louder than ever.

The reasons why this well-intentioned Act failed to produce the objects of its authors are not difficult to discover.

The authors of the Act either mistook what the Irish tenant wanted, or, not finding it expedient to state their object openly, they attempted to attain it indirectly and circuitously—a mode of legislation which generally makes matters worse than they were before. What the tenants wanted was to be left in quiet occupation of their holdings, to secure which they were willing to pay, and often did pay, high, nay, extravagant rents. The measure which they agitated for was that so long as they paid the rent they should not be disturbed in their possession; the Act passed in 1870 merely made it expensive for the landlord to turn them out. The compensation for disturbance, and compensation for improvements, were not what the tenant wanted; this pecuniary compensation was nothing in comparison to the loss of his home, and the destruction of his business; a sum of money in hand was no adequate compensation to him, for he knew only two modes of using it, either in stocking a farm, or lodging it in a bank upon the security of a deposit receipt. It was doubtless imagined that the landlord would be deterred from serving notices to quit, by the amount of the compensation for disturbance, as statesmen have endeavoured to exclude an article by attaching to its importation a prohibitory duty. In the case of a prohibitory tariff its object is defeated, if wealthy men are willing to pay an extravagant price, or if the market price of the article rise so high that it can be sold at a profit after payment of the duty. If the landlord were wealthy and wanted the land, he asserted his legal rights, and was ready to pay the legal penalty; the tenant lost his holding and got such damages as he might. Supposing the landlord to be not only wealthy, but generous to his tenants, the matter would be worked out in somewhat the following fashion. The landlord wishing to get up possession, offers to the tenant a sum of money to surrender his interests, which the latter, indignant as Naboth at the proposal to purchase his vineyard, unhesitatingly refuses; notice to quit follows, and then an ejectment process; the tenant files his claim for compensation, putting down for disturbance the maximum rate, and claiming compensation for everything done on the lands as an improvement; whether a cow shed was erected, or an old house pulled down; fences built up or ditches levelled; bog reclaimed or bog cut out; everything is an improvement, and not an ounce of bone dust has been put into the lands for the last seven years, nor has a cow crossed the field during that period, which is not entered under the head of unexhausted manure. When the 'land' case comes on, the landlord's witnesses, marshalled by an excited agent, are equal to the occasion; every improvement alleged by the tenant is proved to have been detrimental to the value of the holding; anything erected by the tenant is described as no better than a hovel; anything which he has pulled down as substantial and useful; the ditches levelled were most necessary for drainage; the fences erected render the lands useless for agriculture; thus the battle of evidence sways to and fro, until the County Court Judge, acting upon his own knowledge of things in general, more than the evidence given in the case, makes a decision, liberal in intention, but which often leaves the tenant with less money in his pocket than if he had accepted the terms which he might originally have obtained.[1]

When the market for land is rising, and the tenants begin to compete against each other, the costs of the ejectment, and the compensation payable under the Act, are frequently advanced by the incoming tenant, who has undertaken also to pay an increased rent; the consciousness that their present distress is largely due to their own struggles to secure the possession of lands explains the great unpopularity of anyone who is found in possession of a farm which had belonged to another.[2]

---

[1] In the case of Tracey *v.* Dick, in the county of Wicklow, the landlord offered the tenant 600*l.* in full for all his claims to compensation; this the tenant refused, and filed a land claim for 1300*l.*; after six days' examination of witnesses, the tenant was awarded 350*l.*, and 26*l.* for his costs. The actual cash expenditure, chiefly for witnesses, was five times the amount of the taxed costs.

[2] When a tenant demands a reduction of his rent, the question whether he has in fact any equitable or moral ground for such a demand turns upon the circumstances under which he has obtained possession of the land subject to the rent, as it must be conceded that the mere inconvenience or impossibility of the payment is in itself no ground for such remission, if the tenant is to continue in possession.

1. If the tenant, holding originally at a less rent, has been gradually forced to pay an ever-increasing rent by the constantly-repeated threat of a notice to quit, the landlord, if insisting upon payment, should receive the same and no more assistance from a court of law, than is given to the moneylender who has taken advantage of the distress of his debtor to coerce him into unreasonable and oppressive stipulations.

2. If, however, the tenant has obtained possession by

The Act, by the scale adopted for compensation for disturbance, rendered it the interest of the landlord to consolidate small holdings and to let his land to large farmers only. That it was advantageous to the public that the very small holdings of poor tenants should be diminished, was by all admitted, and it was perhaps one of the objects of the Act to increase the average acreage of farms; but the immediate effect of the 3rd section was to render it more difficult for the small farmer without capital, when once evicted, to obtain a new holding. The landlord was also forced by these provisions of the Act, to eject all subtenants upon the determination of the interest of the middleman.

Compensation for improvements, payable at the determination of a lease, is felt by the owners of the land as inconvenient and oppressive. It

---

himself offering to pay the rent in question, he cannot plead the mistake in his own estimate of the value, nor his present inability to pay, unless he be willing to rescind the bargain by giving up possession. That such a tenant should insist upon retaining his farm at a reduced rent, is as absurd as that a merchant, who has resold a cargo at a loss, should require an abatement from the original vendor.

3. If the tenant's inability to pay arise from his having given an extravagant price to his predecessor in the farm, he has clearly no moral right to ask for a reduction; by the price which he paid voluntarily for his interest in the letting, he has given emphatic testimony to the fact that the rent was below the market value; and if he was induced to pay more than the true value, his equity is against the last tenant —the assignor—not against the owner of the land.

may be answered that for the money which they pay to the outgoing tenant they receive a full equivalent in the increased value of their land. Landlords, however, from the very nature of their property, have, in proportion to their income, less ready money than any other class in the community, and if the law require a man who has no capital to purchase the property of his outgoing tenant, it does not much diminish his embarrassment to be assured that the improvements in question may possibly be worth the money. A wealthy or reckless tenant may so improve the premises as to render it impossible for a landlord with but a moderate income to regain possession. Instances of the most extravagant claims for improvements are of not unfrequent occurrence, and the determination of the lease is but too often the commencement of litigation. Landlords therefore desire to let lands to those only the value of whose aggregate holdings falls within the 12th section, and to insist upon the tenant covenanting himself out of the Act. Forms of leases, varying more or less in other particulars, but containing this material proviso, are in extensive, if not universal, use in all large and well managed estates, and to this extent the Act of 1870 has failed to have any practical result.

The right to compensation for disturbance and improvements having given to the tenants a certain marketable interest in their holdings, they suddenly acquired a security which enabled them to borrow money and obtain credit which they had never before enjoyed. Numerous competing branch banks were opened in insignificant country towns, and general dealers pressed their goods upon the farmers' families. During the prosperous years which preceded the present distress the farmers incurred debts to such an extent that, when the subsequent harvest proved deficient, they found their credit already exhausted, and therefore could not obtain money at the very date at which they might have legitimately applied for loans. Thus the farmer who in 1879 had a valuable interest in his farm and a stake in the country, but had also, unfortunately, an overdue bill in the bank, and a balance against him on his account with the shopkeeper, found himself in a worse position than he had been in before 1870, when his inability to borrow protected him against debt.

The Act of 1870 professed to obtain for the tenant security of tenure; its only effect was that, when the market value of land was rising, it slightly delayed the date at which the landlord would find it profitable to evict the tenant. The authors of the Act considered that the tenant should be satisfied if he obtained a lease for thirty-one years, and attempted to secure him this advantage by making it the interest of the landlord to grant a lease for that term; but the sections introduced to compel the landlord to grant such a lease made it the interest of the tenant to decline to accept it; his tenancy from year to year might last for an indefinite period, and could not then be determined without compensation, but—the chances against any particular tenant being evicted were very great—the acceptance by the tenant of a lease fixed a date, however remote, at which the tenure would determine, without compensation, except for permanent improvements; and he therefore considered a lease for a fixed number of years as little else than a deferred notice to quit.

The Act of 1870 was founded upon a misconception of what the tenant desired, and created hopes which it failed to realise.

The first and second sections of the Act propose to deal with the usages prevalent in the province of Ulster, or elsewhere, which were known under the denomination of the Ulster Tenant Right. No uniform custom of tenant right existed in Ulster, but upon various estates there had grown up certain modes of dealing with reference to the letting of land, which, although differing in details, resembled each other in their leading characteristics. Prior to the date of the Act, these usages were not recognised by the law, and were enforced only by the pressure of public opinion; they were, in fact, customs, not laws, and in the most rudimentary condition. The Act did not attempt to define the nature of such usages, but made *the custom of the estate* an implied term in any contract of letting; it extended to the usages existing upon estates in Ulster the rule already applied by the English Courts, to what was known in England as the 'Customs of the Country.' For a 'Custom of the Country' to be recognised by the English Courts it need not be proved to have existed from time immemorial, but may be established upon proof of a usage reasonable and certain in its nature, and generally acted on in a particular district. The principle upon which the English judges acted is fully explained in the judgment of Baron Parke, in the case of Hutton *v.* Warren, 1 Mee & Welsb, 466 : 'It has been long settled that in commercial transactions extrinsic evidence of custom and usage is admissible to annex incidents to written contracts in matters with respect to which they are silent. The same rule has also been applied to contracts in other transactions of life, in which known usages have been established and prevailed; and this has been done upon the principle of presumption that, in such transactions, the parties did not mean to express in writing the whole of the contract by which they intended to be bound, but to contract with reference to those known usages. Whether such a relaxation of the Common Law is wisely applied where formal instruments have been entered into, and particularly leases under seal, may well be doubted; but the contrary has been established by such authority, and the relations between landlord and tenant have been so long regulated upon the supposition that all customary obligations, not altered by the contract, are to remain in force, that it is too late to pursue a contrary course, and it would be productive of much inconvenience if this practice were now to be disturbed.'

The Irish Law Courts have been blamed for not treating the Ulster usages as 'customs of the country,' but wrongly so, for the latter are essentially different in their nature from all forms of Ulster Tenant Right; they were all merely conversant with the due cultivation of the land and were upheld as being beneficial for both landlord and tenant. They were all customs by which the tenant, upon leaving, was entitled to be compensated for something which he had done to the land by which he had increased its value; as, for instance, a custom by which the tenant was entitled to the way-going crop, to an allowance for unexhausted manures, for straw or manure left on the farm, for money spent on drainage or fencing. All these are matters for which a landlord, on making a letting from year to year, might reasonably contract to compensate the tenant for upon the determination of the tenancy; but a custom, such as that of Ulster, to pay to the tenant the value of his occupancy upon the legal determination of his tenancy, was one contradictory to the nature of the estate created, and excluded by the terms of the contract itself. The views expressed by the Irish Judges upon this subject are fully justified by the judgments of the House of Lords in the case of Ramsden v. Dyson, L. R., 1 H. of L. 129.

The nature of the Ulster Tenant Right will appear from the following judgments of the learned Judge of the County Court of Fermanagh: 'What are the characteristics and meaning of tenant right? It may be divided into three phases. The first is that the tenant may remain in possession of his holding, whether he hold under a lease or otherwise, subject, on the fall of the lease, to a revision of the rent, and subject, in case there is no lease, to a periodical and reasonable revision of the rent. The tenant is to remain in possession in this way, and under these circumstances; and this is tenant right. The next stage of tenant right is this. Suppose the tenant not to be remaining in possession, but that he is parting with his interest in the property by transfer or assignment. The usage in that case was that the tenant should be at liberty to do so, but that the landlord at the same time should have a right of veto—the right to say, "I won't accept that man as my tenant." This part of the tenant right was simply that the tenant should have the liberty of substituting a man equally good with himself as the future occupier of the holding. In connection with this we are to inquire what was the price to be paid to the tenant. The outgoing tenant pocketed the price of his interest in the property, a sum which was differently regulated on different estates. In some cases the landlord fixed it; on other estates it was limited to a certain number of years' purchase; and on others the old tenant was freely allowed to sell by public auction. All these apparent differences do not alter the custom; they are not—to speak in the language of logicians—the essential attributes, but merely the accidents. When these rules are permanently established on the estate, I would say that they are absolutely binding. The next stage or phase of tenant right is—Suppose the old tenant is remaining in possession, or suppose that he is not selling, but that the landlord is taking the holding to himself; if the landlord takes the land into his own hands, it is a question of law whether we have the authority to make the landlord pay the full marketable price—whether we are not to restrain him by an injunction to let the tenant sell.'—(Jolly v. Archdale, Chapters on Tenant Right Land Act, and Reports by Donnell, 327).

'Common to all the usages or tenant right customs there are five leading features, which may be termed the essential attributes, viz.:—

'1st. The right or custom in general of yearly tenants, or those deriving through them, to continue in undisturbed possession as long as they act properly and pay their rents.

'2nd. The correlative right of the landlord perpetually to raise the rent, so as to give him a just, fair, and full participation in the increased value of the lands, but not so as to extinguish the tenant's interest by imposing a rack-rent.

'3rd. The usage or custom of the yearly tenants to sell their interest, if they do not wish to continue in possession, or if they become unable to pay the rent.

'4th. The correlative right of the landlord to be consulted, and to exercise a potential voice in the approval or disapproval of the proposed assignee.

'5th. The liability of the landlord, if taking land for his own purpose from a tenant, to pay the tenant the fair value of his tenant right.

'These five elements I have found existing in every usage or tenant right custom that was proved before me; and the special characteristics proved, in relation to the tenant right recognised on particular estates, for the most part had reference to some limitation or restriction affecting the tenant in his right of sale, or to the mode adopted by the landlord for asserting his rights under the 2nd and 4th of the above heads. When therefore a claim of tenant right is made by the tenant, and either its existence or its character is disputed by the landlord, the controversy must be determined by the evidence given on either side.' (Graham *v.* The Earl of Erne id. p. 405.)

The legal effect of the Act of 1870 in regard to the Ulster Tenant Right was very clearly put by the County Court Judge for the county of Down:

'Whatever practice prevailed for any reasonable time previous to the passing of the Act, and not imposed in contemplation of the Act, was the tenant right legalised upon that estate, no matter what the tenant right might be in the district round about.' (Kevan *v.* Lord De Ros, *ib.* p. 267.)

The essential point in the Ulster Tenant Right was undoubtedly the mode in which the 'fair rent' to be paid by the tenant was ascertained; it was fixed not by open competition but by valuation. The revaluation for the purpose of fixing the rent at the determination of a lease, or at any time during a tenancy from year to year, was always made by a professional valuator, or at least one in whom both parties had confidence, who valued the farm having reference to the fair value of the ground, exclusive of buildings and tenant's improvements.

The Ulster usages not only recognised rights as between the landlord and his immediate tenant, but as between him and the subtenants upon the expiration of the interest of the middleman.

The custom upon this point is thus summed up by Mr. Donnell (Chapters on Tenant Right, &c., p. 79.)

1. On the determination of a non-occupying middleman's lease, the subtenants in occupation are received as tenants of the head landlord at fair customary rents.

2. This allowed them a tenant right interest equal to that usually prevalent in the district

3. If it was necessary to consolidate the holdings, the outgoing subtenants were permitted to sell their tenant right to the continuing subtenants, or to receive from them the full value thereof.

4. If the landlord, for the purpose of enlarging his demesne, ejected any of the subtenants, he paid therefor a fair tenant right compensation.

The obvious objection to the Ulster Customs is that an incoming tenant loses the pecuniary advantages incident to the hiring of land, being compelled to sink a portion of his capital in the purchase of the interest of the outgoing tenant, and his means of profitably working his farm being *pro tanto* diminished.

The preceding analysis of the Act of 1870 and the Ulster Custom is sufficient to show how much more secure and satisfactory is the position of the tenant under the latter than under the former. The custom was forced upon the landlords simply by the pressure of the public opinion of an intelligent and industrious peasantry; and, like all popular customs, it precisely meets the necessities of the case because it was produced and developed by them.

The few and simple rules in which the Ulster Custom may be expressed contrast favourably with the bewildering sections, subsections, provisions, and exceptions in which the Act of the 33–34 Vict. ch. 46 is hopelessly entangled.

It is proposed by some to define the Ulster

Custom by statute, and to extend it to the rest of Ireland. By such an enactment the condition of the Irish tenant, and that of the Irish landlord also, would be much improved, but it is far from certain that by such a course anyone would be satisfied or the agitation stayed.

Almost all who at present discuss the Irish land question profess each to be possessed of the infallible remedy by which the Irish tenants can be transformed from a revolutionary proletariat into a wealthy and conservative peasantry; before, however, anyone undertakes to construct a statute upon the subject it might be advisable to consider and devise distinct answers to the following questions. We assume that it is not proposed to confiscate the rights of individuals or to recast the social system, by the thorough and drastic measures available in such a universal overturning of society as the French Revolution. Upon this assumption the queries annexed have been drawn up as follows, viz.:—

Whether or not it must be admitted that the doctrines of the political economists as to the free trade in land, when applied to the relations of the Irish landlord and tenant, have proved inapplicable, if not actually mischievous, so that every approximation to the Civil or French Law is discovered to be injurious to the condition of the peasantry and the peace of the country; and, if so, whether, having regard to the future of the country, it is expedient to reform our laws so as to assimilate them to those in use among nations of an inferior social development?

Whether the letting of land should or should not be classed as a sub-denomination of and subject to the general rules applicable to cases of hiring; and, further, whether the law of landlord and tenant in Ireland should continue to be founded upon the basis of contract, or should henceforth to a greater or less extent be openly referable to status solely?

If it be considered advisable that some tenancies should be regulated by rules depending on status and not on contract, upon what principle, and with reference to what standard, are tenancies to be divided into those of status and those of contract?

Whether in the case of tenancies which are to be left to contract it would not be advisable (having regard to the 12th section) to repeal the Act of 33–34 Vict. ch. 46, and to substitute a short and definite statement of all the agreements necessarily implied by law, as is done in the Code Napoléon, leaving it to the parties to contract themselves out of them as they desire?

Whether it is not the vital point, in all tenancies resting upon status, that the rent should be fixed otherwise than by bargain between the parties; and, if so, how and in what manner shall the rent to be paid by any such tenant be assessed, and also by what authority or with reference to what standard shall the rents of existing tenants be reduced or raised, so as to be made uniform, and also when and how shall this rent from time to time be readjusted?

If the rent of land is to be fixed with reference to the gross produce, whether by the 'gross produce' is to be understood the present gross produce of the land under a slovenly and careless system of farming, or the possible gross produce of the land if skilfully and carefully tilled?

What do we mean by the terms 'security of tenure,' and 'fixity of tenure'? Under such a system, what would be the rights and duties of the landlord—and what those of the tenant?

If fixity of tenure (the right to possession for so long as the rent is paid) be granted to the tenants up to a certain maximum, whether it may not be expedient, in the interest of the public, to fix a minimum also below which fixity of tenure should not be granted?

Whether the fixity of tenure to be granted shall be confined to certain only of the existing tenancies, or be hereafter acquired by any person to whom land may be let, irrespective of the expressed terms of the letting, or in default of any express agreement?

Whether tenants who shall acquire fixity of tenure should be allowed to sublet the land or erect additional dwellings thereupon, thus creating a new and worse class of landlords; and also whether middlemen should be entitled to fixity of tenure, inasmuch as under no definition of a fair rent could they be entitled to a profit rent?

Whether tenants who shall acquire fixity of tenure should or should not be allowed to assign parts of their holdings, or subdivide same by their will or otherwise, inasmuch as in the former case the unrestricted increase of population will rapidly deteriorate the condition of the peasantry?

Whether tenants who shall acquire fixity of tenure should or should not be permitted to mortgage, charge, or incumber their interest in the perpetuity?

Whether tenants who shall acquire fixity of tenure should be punishable for waste, or should be placed in the same position as tenants in fee farm, under the 23–24 Vict. ch. 154, sec. 25?

Whether a tenant who shall acquire fixity of tenure should be bound to keep buildings, &c., in order, and to cultivate the land in a proper and husbandlike manner; and, if so, how can he be compelled to do so save by the forfeiture of his interest?

Whether the tenant's fixity of tenure should be a right against his own landlord (*in personam*), or against the public (*in rem*)?

If for the public benefit the landlord be deprived of the power of freely dealing with his land, whether he is entitled to any, and, if so, what compensation? and upon what principle should it be assessed?

If a landlord for the public benefit be required to accept, and not permitted to demand more than, the 'fair rent,' whether he should or should not be guaranteed by the State the punctual payment of such 'fair rent'?

Whether to the landlord or the tenant possessing fixity of tenure should belong subsequent accidental increments of value?

Whether the grant to a tenant of fixity of tenure at a 'fair rent' is not merely a circumlocution for the conveyance of the fee simple to the tenant charged with a rent charge for the landlord? and, if so—

Whether the landlord should not have all the powers for the recovery of this 'fair rent,' which are usually given to annuitants or mortgagees by specific agreement or statute? and also—

Whether the landlord should under these circumstances pay all the county cess, and one half of the poor rate, otherwise than other annuitants or remembrancers?

Whether the owner of the rent should have any, and, if so, what process for the recovery of the rent, and whether a power of recovering the rent does not ultimately involve the disturbance of the tenant, by an ejectment for the non-payment of rent or sale of his interest?

Whether there cannot be devised some practical and inexpensive mode whereby the tenant may be enabled, without danger to the rights of third parties, to buy up the rent charged upon his holding?

If the general principle and nature of the reform to be effected in the law of landlord and tenant have been once determined upon, the following points *as to the form of the statute* will remain for consideration :—

(1) Whether it is not advantageous that all the legal rules as to the hiring of land should be included in one consistent and intelligible Act? and that no attempt be made to carry out any proposed reform by the process of engrafting new and isolated rules, exceptions, and provisions upon a series of statutes already sufficiently confused and illogical? and whether it would not also be advantageous that any new land law, besides being complete in itself, should be drawn up in such language, form, and manner, that the landlords and tenants in Ireland (or at least such of them as are reasonably educated) should, like the inhabitants of Continental Europe and America, be able, without professional assistance, to discover their respective rights and duties? and—

(2) Whether it is not more advantageou that the additional rights and advantages (if any) to be given to the tenant should be expressed in affirmative and distinct language, and not obliquely and impliedly introduced by the restriction of the exercise by the landlords of rights still admitted to be legal?

APPENDIX.

POPULAR ERRORS AS TO IRISH LAW.

IN all countries in which the law has been codified, every ordinarily educated person either knows, or can easily ascertain, the rules of the law applicable to any specific legal relation. The English and Irish law has never been codified, nor indeed any serious attempt ever made to effect this most desirable object, which has, during the last half century, been continuously postponed to political measures or party objects. Thus the English public have become so habituated to consider their law as a mystery, and its rules the antithesis to the principles of common-sense, that they are contented to remain ignorant of its provisions, and to hand over the entire management of their legal affairs to their solicitors.

The general principles of English law are neither obscure nor illogical when they are mastered, but the authorities are scattered through innumerable reports and Acts of Parliament, so that laymen cannot easily even make inquiries as to the matter, and of the professional students who attempt to master it few ever arrive at any satisfactory result.

It is not therefore to be expected that those who deal with social questions, and attempt the reform of obvious abuses, should as a preliminary undertake an exhaustive study of the law; but it may be fairly hoped that before they appeal to the public for the introduction of a new and beneficial law, or the repeal of some old and mischievous rule, they should at least ascertain whether the law which they desire to introduce has not been for years on the face of the statute book, or whether that which they desire to repeal had any existence at all. It is also often very useful to consider whether the law complained of is peculiar to this country, or of common use in all civilised nations, in which case there is a strong presumption in its favour; and, further, those who bring forward cases of individual hardship may be expected to inquire whether the sufferer could not have got full relief if he had observed the directions of the existing law, or applied to the ordinary tribunals; and also, whether, although confident he was an injured man, it is not possible that he was utterly in the wrong himself from the very commencement.

We desire here to give a few examples of the extraordinary errors as to the existing Irish land law common in books or speeches dealing with the Irish land question. In the well-known work, 'Land Systems, and Industrial Economy of Ireland, England, and Continental Countries,' by Mr. Cliffe Leslie, p. 118, there occurs the following passage: 'Twenty years ago, Dr. Hancock applied himself to discover the cause of the absence of trees; and the cause he discovered is admirably illustrated by a communication to Lord Devon's Commission, which we beg our readers to study, not for its direct application to trees only, but for all the analogous impediments to improvement and cultivation it suggests: "Under the encouragement (says the writer) which I conceived the laws in force afforded to me, I planted trees extensively in lands which I held for a terminable lease. They are mine, I said, to all intents and purposes. I took the best care of them, fenced and protected them, and of course paid rent, &c., for the land they grew on for a number of years, and I considered them not only as a shelter and ornament to my place, but as a crop which I was raising on my farm for the benefit of myself and my family. But *legibus aliter visum est.* On taking out a renewal of my lease, it appeared that my crop of timber, most of which had been growing for nearly forty years, while I paid the rent, could not be mine by law. Let me do the landlord no injustice. He had no disposition to possess himself of my trees. He felt that they ought to be mine. But the only lease he could give me was one by which I not only could never call one branch of the trees I planted, protected, and paid for, mine, but by which I am liable to severe penalties if I cut a switch off any of them. My Lord, 'tis monstrous! Will the face of the country improve under such a law? Shall I be mad enough now to begin planting again, and leave a copy of the statement for my son, with *da capo* written at the end of it, against the expiration of my present lease? No, I will grow furze, or heath, or brambles, but I won't grow timber." '

It is immaterial to observe that neither under the Roman, French, nor English law would a tenant who planted trees upon his farm acquire the property in them; but what is very important to the question is that, under *the Irish law, a tenant who plants trees during the term of his lease can acquire a property in them.*

By the Irish Statute, 23-24 George III. ch. 39,

it is enacted that any tenant for life or lives, or *any tenant for years exceeding fourteen years unexpired*, who shall plant any trees, shall be entitled to cut, sell, and dispose of the same, at any time during the term ; provided that any tenant, so planting, shall, within twelve calendar months after such planting, lodge with the clerk of the peace of the county, or county of a city, where such plantation shall be made, an affidavit sworn before some justice of the peace of the county, reciting the number and kinds of the trees planted, and the name of the lands in the form prescribed by the Act (section 2). The trees in question therefore were the property of the tenant, if he had taken the trouble to register them ; but having omitted to do so, he had none save himself to blame. It is notorious that the tenant's interest in registered timber is a property perfectly well known in Ireland, and frequently sold and purchased in the same manner as any personal chattel. The history of the peculiar Irish legislation upon this subject is set out at length in Furlong's Landlord and Tenant, Book IV. chap. 6.

In the 76th page of the same work, speaking of the embarrassments caused to tenants by the existing law, there occurs this passage : ' The first sentence of Mr. Furlong's treatise on the " Law of Landlord and Tenant in Ireland " is "The common law regulating the enjoyment of real property, both in England and Ireland, is founded upon and governed by the principles of the feudal system." ' Such a statement in 1870, the date of Mr. Cliffe Leslie's essay, ten years after the passing of the Irish Act of 1860, which swept all feudal ideas out of the legal relation of landlord and tenant in Ireland, is certainly remarkable. This reference in the essay naturally suggests the following ob-

APPENDIX. 119

servation: the passage in question does occur as the first sentence in the original edition of Furlong's well-known work published in 1845; but in the second edition, published in 1869, the year before the date of Mr. Cliffe Leslie's essay, the passage is postponed to some preliminary definitions, and is not the first sentence of the work; hence we may infer that the edition used by the author of the essay in question was the old one, not corrected as to the statutes passed between 1845 and 1870.

In the same work, page 52, occurs the following passage: 'An illustration must be given of the obstructions which the land laws under which Ireland has been placed have opposed to the enterprise and prosperity of its people in other ways. "About fifteen years ago," Dr. Hancock relates in his treatise on the 'Impediments to the Prosperity of Ireland,' "an enterprising capitalist was anxious to build a flax-mill in the north of Ireland, as a change had become necessary in the linen trade from hand-spinning to mill-spinning. He selected as the site for his mill a place in a poor but populous district, situated on a navigable river, and in the immediate vicinity of extensive turf bogs. The capitalist applied to the landlord for a lease of fifty acres for a mill site, labourers' village, and his own residence, and of fifty acres of bog, as it was proposed to use turf as the fuel for the steam-engines for the mill. The landlord was most anxious to encourage an enterprise so well calculated to improve the estate. An agreement was concluded, but when the flax-spinner consulted his legal adviser he discovered that the law prevented the landlord from carrying out the very liberal terms he had agreed to. He was bound by settlement to let for the best rent only; the longest lease he could grant was for three lives, or thirty-one years. Such a lease, however, at the full rent of the lands, was quite too short to secure the flax-spinner in laying out his capital in building; the statute enabling tenants[1] to lease for mill sites only allowing leases for three acres. The mill was not built, and mark the consequence. Some twenty miles from the spot alluded to, the flax-spinner had land in which he could get a perpetual interest; there he laid out his thousands; there he has for the last fifteen years given employment to hundreds of labourers, and has earned money. The poor but populous district continues to be populous, but, if anything, poorer than it was. During the past seasons of distress, the people of that district suffered much from want of occupation, the landlords' rents were worse paid out of it than from any other part of his estate. Could there be a stronger case to prove how much the present state of Ireland arises from the state of the law?"'

The essay from which this passage was taken was published in 1868, and reprinted in 1870; yet there is not therein any reference to the Settled Estates Act of 1856, which gave the Court of Chancery the power to lease lands 'for a building for ninety-nine years, or when the Court shall be satisfied that it is the usual custom of the district, and beneficial to the inheritance, to grant building leases for longer terms, then for such term as the Court shall direct' (19–20 Vict. ch. 120, section 2), nor to the notorious fact that the Court has exercised its power of granting leases for very lengthy terms for the very purpose of the erection of linen manufactories, and that applications for leasing

[1] This must mean 'enabling *tenants for life* to lease,' and the Act referred to is the Irish Act of the 25th Geo. III. ch. 62.

powers under the Act in question are of constant occurrence. An order of the Master of the Rolls made under this Act authorising a lease for a very long term for the erection of a linen manufactory, in the case of the estate of the Earl of Charlemont, may be inspected in the office of the Chancery Registrars. Again, in the 77th page of the same work occurs this passage. 'What is more important: a tenant for years has not the right of ownership, as was afterwards experienced in the very case before us. The capitalist accepted a lease for 999 years; although diverted from his original design with respect to the ground. *In putting it to a different purpose he proceeded to level an eminence, and to carry away the gravel for use elsewhere.* But the law of landlord and tenant says:—"If a tenant opens pits for the purpose of raising stone or waste, it will be waste." And this being the law the landlord actually obtained an injunction to restrain the tenant's proceedings, and mulcted him in damages.' It can scarcely be gravely alleged that the Irish law is exceptional and unreasonable which forbids one who has hired the use of the superficies of land, for a limited term, to destroy the corpus of the demised premises by carrying off and appropriating the gravel on the land, an act the result of which probably in most cases would be that, when the 'eminence' of valuable gravel had been disposed of, the premises would be thrown back on the landlord's hands in the condition of a gravel pit filled with water. The next paragraph is also as remarkable: 'Once more, in another county, the very same capitalist opened an iron mine by arrangement with the lord of the soil, and commenced works on an extensive scale. *The landlord then demanded terms to which he was not entitled by his contract;* but the price of Irish iron has not been high enough of late years to defray the cost of a Chancery suit in addition to the costs of production, and delay, worry, and anxiety are not inducements to industrial enterprise; so the iron works were suspended.' It is insinuated here that the Irish law is mischievously defective because it does not prevent a landlord from making claims as to the merits of which we have no means of judging, and that Courts can do no more than deal with disputes when they have arisen; and, again, it is ignored that if the landlord had demanded terms to which he was not entitled under his contract, he would have had to pay the costs of the suit. As to the peculiar costs and delay of the Chancery proceeding, it may be added that the old and expensive practice of Chancery had been abolished in 1851, and a very simple, cheap, and (when accounts had not to be taken) expeditious course of procedure then existed in that Court. It may not unreasonably be conjectured that the capitalist who took so peculiar a view of his rights as a lessee for years, perhaps fell into some similar error as to his rights under his mining lease.

As to the *Irish* law of waste, Mr. Cliffe Leslie makes very remarkable statements, and uses very strong language. Thus, in page 107:—

'*A legislature of landlords, devising a code of laws for Ireland, has thought only of the landlord; and the ground has been cursed for his sake.* Does anyone need further illustration of the fundamental policy of that code? He will find it in a passage of the standard treatise on "The Law of Landlord and Tenant in Ireland," defining what waste is in the eye of the law— "A tenant has no right to alter the nature of the land demised, by converting ancient pasture into arable land, or arable land into woodland, or by enclosing and cultivating waste land included in the demise, &c." Is it not rightly called a law of waste? To keep the land of the island unchanged, unchangeable, and unimproved alike in its own condition and its ownership, to keep the world standing still from age to age, and therefore tumbling to decay,' &c., &c.

The passage in Furlong is to be found in the 657th page in the old edition; if reference be made to the footnotes of Mr. Furlong's work, we find no trace of a code of laws devised for Ireland by a legislature of landlords; Mr. Furlong does not refer to any Irish statute in support of his statements, nor, indeed, could he, as there never were any such enactments, as anyone can easily ascertain by reference to 'Oulton's Index of the Irish Statutes,' p. 795, title 'Waste'; but he does refer to no less than seventeen reported cases, *all of which without exception are English*, and all turn upon the simple principle that he who hires an article cannot destroy the article hired, during the period of the hiring, but must return it in the same state in which he received it.

This selection of passages from Mr. Cliffe Leslie is not to be taken as proving that upon this subject he is peculiarly inaccurate; his writings have been made use of because they have naturally, on account of the earnestness and great literary ability of the author, acquired a large circulation, and exercised much influence upon public opinion. As to the less known and less careful writers upon this subject, we can only say—*Quia si in viridi ligno hæc faciunt, in arido quid fiet?*

An instance of the extraordinary manner in which the plainest legal principles are ignored occurs in the letter of the 'Special Correspondent of the *Standard*, of the 30th December, 1879.

'He (Lord Sligo) has the reputation of being the only large landlord in Mayo who has raised his rent since the passing of the Land Act; and there is no resisting the evidence that this has been done in some cases to the extent of 50 per cent., on holdings in which it was declared emphatically that the tenant had made all the improvements which were the justification for the advance, the landlord never having contributed a shilling in any shape or form. So far as I could gather, the form in which these improvements were effected, so that it became possible, as it was put to me, for the landlord " to confiscate the capital of his tenants" was this: most of the small holdings are conterminous with large tracts of waste, mountain, or bog land, and the small farmers in their spare time set to work to reclaim portions of these. On the Sligo estate this practice, which is common all over the west of Ireland, has been followed; but the agent has had a sharp eye on such improvements, and instead of the equitable rule which seems to prevail over the Dillon estates, on the Roscommon side of the county, of leaving the improver to enjoy what he has thus created during his tenancy, the landlord has stepped in and insisted on a share—and, as some insisted, the lion's share—the moment there is anything to divide.'

The correctness of the statement is immaterial; as is the meanness or generosity of an owner of property in asserting his rights. The facts of the case, stripped of rhetoric, stand thus. A hires of B the use for a limited period of (say) ten acres at a certain rent, and, having been put into possession of the ten acres agreed upon, enters upon and appropriates the ten adjoining acres, and cultivates for his own profit these second ten acres, to which he has no title whatsoever. The legal bearings of the case would turn upon the following points: (1) Whether the tenant wilfully trespassed upon and wrongfully occupied land which he knew was not his own; in this case he was a wrongdoer from the first, and has no legal *locus standi*. But (2) if the tenant entered upon and improved these lands under a mistake as to his rights (whether referred to custom or otherwise), and the landlord, with notice of the tenant's reclamation and improvements, stood by, intending to appropriate to himself the tenant's expenditure, he would be restrained by an injunction from the perpetration of such a fraud (see O'Fay *v.* Burke, 8 Ir. Ch. p. 518).

If we vary the rank and position of the landlord and tenant, there will be no doubt as to the rule of law to be applied to such a transaction; and upon this subject the following case, the evidence of which is of record in the Court of Chancery, may be safely referred to. By a lease of the 7th of May, 1806, H.M. demised to H.U., the lands of Cloonasea in the King's County, containing 155 Irish acres (251a. 0r. 10p. English), for 21 years, at the rent of 80$l.$ Irish (73$l.$ 16$s.$ 11$\frac{1}{4}d.$ English), with a quoties toties covenant for renewal. The lease was renewed from time to time, down to the year 1869. The representatives of H.M. in 1872 obtained from the Church Commissioners a grant in fee of the lands in question, with others, upon payment of the sum of 2860$l.$ 19$s.$ 4$d.$, and subject to the perpetual head rent of 407$l.$ 1$s.$ 7$d.$

The lessee under the lease of 1806 sub-let the lands to various under-tenants, who commenced and carried out a series of encroachments upon the adjoining lands.

In 1875 the representatives of H.U. instituted proceedings in the Court of Chancery, to obtain a sub-fee farm grant of the land then in the occupation of their under-tenants and the rent of which they were in receipt of. In the proceedings under the petition in question, it was proved by the representatives of H.M., the original lessor, and admitted by the petitioners, that the latter, by their under-tenants, were in possession of not less than 266 Irish acres (430a. 3r. 17p. English), of which 111 Irish acres (179a. 3r. 7p. English) had been acquired solely by encroachment or 'reclamation of adjoining lands'; by whatever name it is called, the fact is the same. (Before the V.C.; Ussher, petitioner; Balfour and others, respondents. Petition filed the 22nd May, 1875.)

If it be desirable that whoever reclaims the waste lands of another should be entitled to the ownership thereof, the principle should be openly stated, and the proposed amendment of the law to that effect prepared, in which the terms 'waste land,' and 'reclamation' should be intelligibly defined.

As a proof of the extreme ignorance of the present condition of the law of landlord and tenant in Ireland, there cannot be a more remarkable instance than a speech lately delivered by the Venerable Archdeacon O'Connell, the respected and most respectable parish priest of Castleisland. It is to be observed that the object of the speech was to dissuade his parishioners from establishing a branch of the Land League in the district, and that its design and tone were alike moderate and praiseworthy. The Archdeacon naturally prefaced his address by pointing out to his hearers that he himself was sprung from the farming class, and that his own family had as much if not more reason than any of his parishioners to complain of the land laws. 'I am the son of a tenant-farmer myself, and if the sense of a cruel wrong could justify anyone in joining a movement of questionable morality, that justification would be mine. Just thirty years ago my poor father was evicted from a farm held under Baron Foster, after expending not only his capital, but a life-long term of toil and industry, in building, planting, fencing, draining, and otherwise reclaiming what was once a wet swamp. When the lease of that farm expired the rent was raised 25 per cent.; but this was not the worst. In little more than a year after Baron Foster's death, he was served by his son with an ejectment for non-title, and though the rent was punctually paid, and though there was most respectable evidence to prove that there were unexhausted improvements to the value of upwards of 800*l.* effected on the farm, all was of no use. By the decree of a Court of Law, all was confiscated to the use and benefit of this model landlord and his bailiff, who shared with him the spoils of an honest, industrious man. This is but a typical case of the many hundred cases that have occurred *from that day to the present*, throughout the length and breadth of Ireland, and owing to an unjust land system.'—*Irish Times*, 2nd October, 1880.

Let us admit to the fullest extent the correctness of the statement made by this most conscientious clergyman; but we would suggest that if he had taken the trouble to ascertain how the law at present stands, he would have substituted for the last paragraph the following: 'I am happy, however, to inform you that under the amendments in the law which have been effected since that date, such injustice as I have described could not now be perpetrated; for upon the expiration of the first lease my father under the present law would have been entitled to compensation of the full value of his improvements by virtue of the 4th section of the Act of 1870 ; and if the second lease made by Mr. Baron Foster, who was only a tenant for life, were invalid as against his son, the tenant in remainder, my father, by virtue of the 41st section of the Act of 1860, could have recovered damages for the loss of his interest against the representatives of Mr. Baron Foster, by virtue of the covenant for good title and quiet enjoyment which is now implied in all leases.'

There is no need to accumulate further instances, but it is impossible to avoid remarking that the majority of those who have addressed letters to the public papers upon the necessity of a change in the law of landlord and tenant in Ireland assume, as a fact, that a tenant ejected for nonpayment of rent is not entitled to any compensation for improvements, and that the majority of the farms are tenancies at will.

It may be perhaps remarked that the object of this appendix is to suggest that the task of law reform should be left to the lawyers. Far from it—lawyers, as a class, are, of all the community, the least disposed to a reform of an existing system; the labour which they have expended in mastering its technicalities and unravelling its complexities leads them as a rule to vastly overestimate the value of the information which they have thus acquired; they mistake for jurisprudence 'the logical deduction of one absurdity from another,' and believe what is obscure to be profound.

The amateur law reformer, on the other hand, desirous of remedying a specific evil, is too prone to attribute it to some rule of law which is but a portion of a complex system, and, in total disregard of the rights of third parties, proposes its repeal or suggests some crude enactment which, from its conflict with other rules left unrepealed, the existence of which its author was wholly ignorant of, would produce inextricable confusion and litigation.

He who proposes the enactment of a new law in substitution for one in use should at least be able to state with reasonable clearness the details of the measure which he desires to introduce. A statute cannot be drafted by a stroke of genius, nor its details worked out by the purely logical process of converting the existing rules into their contradictories, after the fashion in which Friar John constructed the regulations of the monastery of Thélème. A good and successful Act of Parliament is prepared after the same fashion as a well-drawn deed. The draftsman must know who are the persons whose rights are to be affected; next clearly understand the reciprocal existing rights of the several parties; then have specific instruction as to what he is desired to accomplish; and finally draft a document intelligible, unambiguous, complete, and harmonious.

Law reform is most successfully accomplished by those who, like Flavius Fimbria, not himself a lawyer, have previously mastered the formulæ of the patricians.

LONDON: PRINTED BY
SPOTTISWOODE AND CO., NEW-STREET SQUARE
AND PARLIAMENT STREET

MESSRS. MACMILLAN & CO.'S PUBLICATIONS.

The IRISH CRISIS, being a narrative of the measures for the Relief of the Distress caused by the Great Irish Famine of 1846-7. By Sir CHARLES TREVELYAN, Bart., K.C.B. 8vo. price 2s. 6d.

WORKS BY THE RIGHT HONOURABLE JOHN BRIGHT, M.P.

SPEECHES on QUESTIONS of PUBLIC POLICY. Edited by J. E. THOROLD ROGERS, M.P. Second Edition. Two vols. 8vo. 25s. With Portrait.

AUTHOR'S POPULAR EDITION. Third Edition. Extra fcp. 8vo. 3s. 6d.

PUBLIC ADDRESSES. Edited by J. E. T. ROGERS, M.P. 8vo. 14s.

SPEECHES on QUESTIONS of PUBLIC POLICY. By RICHARD COBDEN, M.P. Edited by Right Hon. JOHN BRIGHT, M.P., and JAMES E. THOROLD ROGERS, M.P. Extra fcp. 8vo. 3s. 6d.

WORKS BY THE RIGHT HON. HENRY FAWCETT, M.P.

THE ECONOMIC POSITION OF THE BRITISH LABOURER. Extra fcp. 8vo. 5s.

MANUAL of POLITICAL ECONOMY. Fifth Edition, revised and enlarged, with New Chapters on the Depreciation of Silver. Crown 8vo. 12s.

PAUPERISM; its Causes and Remedies. Crown 8vo. 5s. 6d.

SPEECHES ON SOME CURRENT POLITICAL QUESTIONS. 8vo. 10s. 6d.

CONTENTS:—Indian Finance—The Birmingham League—Nine Hours Bill—Election Expenses—Women's Suffrage—Household Suffrage in Counties—Irish University Education, &c.

FREE TRADE and PROTECTION. An Enquiry into the Causes which have retarded the general adoption of Free Trade since its Introduction into England. Third Edition. 8vo. 7s. 6d.

INDIAN FINANCE. Three Essays. With Introduction and Appendix. 8vo. 7s. 6d.

WORKS BY MILLICENT GARRETT FAWCETT.

POLITICAL ECONOMY for BEGINNERS, with Questions. Fourth Edition. 18mo. 2s. 6d.

TALES in POLITICAL ECONOMY. Crown 8vo. 3s.

ESSAYS and LECTURES on POLITICAL and SOCIAL SUBJECTS. By Right Hon. HENRY FAWCETT, M.P., and MILLICENT GARRETT FAWCETT. 8vo. 10s. 6d.

WORKS BY W. T. THORNTON, C.B.,
LATE SECRETARY FOR PUBLIC WORKS IN THE INDIA OFFICE.

A PLEA for PEASANT PROPRIETORS, with the Outlines of a Plan for their Establishment in Ireland. New Edition. Crown 8vo. 7s. 6d.

On LABOUR; its Wrongful Claims and Rightful Dues, Actual Present and Possible Future. Second Edition, revised. 8vo. 14s.

OLD-FASHIONED ETHICS and COMMON-SENSE METAPHYSICS. 8vo. 10s. 6d.

INDIAN PUBLIC WORKS, and COGNATE INDIAN TOPICS. Crown 8vo. 8s. 6d.

The LAND QUESTION, with Particular Reference to England and Scotland. By JOHN MACDONELL, Barrister-at-Law. 8vo. price 10s. 6d.

LAWRENCE BLOOMFIELD in IRELAND; or, the New Landlord. Cheaper Issue, with New Preface. By WILLIAM ALLINGHAM. Fcp. 8vo. 4s. 6d.

COMMENTARIES on the LIBERTY of the SUBJECT, and the LAWS of ENGLAND RELATING to the SECURITY of the PERSON. By JAMES PATERSON, Barrister-at-Law. Cheaper Issue. Two vols. Crown 8vo. 21s.

The LIBERTY of the PRESS, SPEECH and PUBLIC WORSHIP. Being Commentaries on the Liberty of the Subject and the Laws of England. By JAMES PATERSON, Barrister-at-Law. Crown 8vo. 12s.

GUIDE to the STUDY of POLITICAL ECONOMY. By Dr. LUIGI COSSA, Professor in the University in Pavia. Translated from the Second Italian Edition. With a Preface by W. STANLEY JEVONS, F.R.S. Crown 8vo. 4s. 6d.

The ECONOMICS of INDUSTRY. By ALFRED MARSHALL, M.A., Principal of University College, Bristol; and MARY PALEY MARSHALL, late Lecturer at Newnham Hall, Cambridge. Extra fcp. 8vo. 2s. 6d.

London: MACMILLAN & CO.

BEDFORD STREET, STRAND, LONDON, W.C.
December, 1879.

MACMILLAN & Co.'s CATALOGUE of Works in the Departments of History, Biography, Travels, Critical and Literary Essays, Politics, Political and Social Economy, Law, etc.; and Works connected with Language.

HISTORY, BIOGRAPHY, TRAVELS, &c.

Albemarle.—FIFTY YEARS OF MY LIFE. By GEORGE THOMAS, Earl of Albemarle. With Steel Portrait of the first Earl of Albemarle, engraved by JEENS. Third and Cheaper Edition. Crown 8vo. 7s. 6d.

"*The book is one of the most amusing of its class. . . . These reminiscences have the charm and flavour of personal experience, and they bring us into direct contact with the persons they describe.*"—EDINBURGH REVIEW.

Anderson.—MANDALAY TO MOMIEN; a Narrative of the Two Expeditions to Western China, of 1868 and 1875, under Colonel E. B. Sladen and Colonel Horace Browne. By Dr. ANDERSON, F.R.S.E., Medical and Scientific Officer to the Expeditions. With numerous Maps and Illustrations. 8vo. 21s.

"*A pleasant, useful, carefully-written, and important work.*"—ATHENÆUM.

Appleton.—Works by T. G. APPLETON:—

A NILE JOURNAL. Illustrated by EUGENE BENSON. Crown 8vo. 6s.

SYRIAN SUNSHINE. Crown 8vo. 6s.

Arnold (M.)—ESSAYS IN CRITICISM. By MATTHEW ARNOLD. New Edition, Revised and Enlarged. Crown 8vo. 9s.

Arnold (W. T.)—THE ROMAN SYSTEM OF PROVINCIAL ADMINISTRATION TO THE ACCESSION OF CONSTANTINE THE GREAT. Being the Arnold Prize Essay for 1879. By W. T. Arnold, B.A. Crown 8vo. 6s.

Atkinson.—AN ART TOUR TO NORTHERN CAPITALS OF EUROPE, including Descriptions of the Towns, the Museums, and other Art Treasures of Copenhagen, Christiania, Stockholm, Abo, Helsingfors, Wiborg, St. Petersburg, Moscow, and Kief. By J. BEAVINGTON ATKINSON. 8vo. 12s.

Bailey.—THE SUCCESSION TO THE ENGLISH CROWN. A Historical Sketch. By A. BAILEY, M.A., Barrister-at-Law. Crown 8vo. 7s. 6d.

Baker (Sir Samuel W.)—Works by Sir SAMUEL BAKER, Pacha, M.A., F.R.S., F.R.G.S.:—

CYPRUS AS I SAW IT IN 1879. With Frontispiece. 8vo. 12s. 6d.

ISMAILIA: A Narrative of the Expedition to Central Africa for the Suppression of the Slave Trade, organised by Ismail, Khedive of Egypt. With Portraits, Map, and fifty full-page Illustrations by ZWECKER and DURAND. New and Cheaper Edition. With New Preface. Crown 8vo. 6s.

"*A book which will be read with very great interest.*"—TIMES. "*Well written and full of remarkable adventures.*"—PALL MALL GAZETTE. "*Adds another thrilling chapter to the history of African adventure.*"—DAILY NEWS. "*Reads more like a romance.... incomparably more entertaining than books of African travel usually are.*"—MORNING POST.

THE ALBERT N'YANZA Great Basin of the Nile, and Exploration of the Nile Sources. Fifth Edition. Maps and Illustrations. Crown 8vo. 6s.

"*Charmingly written;*" *says the* SPECTATOR, "*full, as might be expected, of incident, and free from that wearisome reiteration of useless facts which is the drawback to almost all books of African travel.*"

THE NILE TRIBUTARIES OF ABYSSINIA, and the Sword Hunters of the Hamran Arabs. With Maps and Illustrations. Sixth Edition. Crown 8vo. 6s.

The TIMES *says:* "*It adds much to our information respecting Egyptian Abyssinia and the different races that spread over it. It contains, moreover, some notable instances of English daring and enterprising skill; it abounds in animated tales of exploits dear to the heart of the British sportsman; and it will attract even the least studious reader, as the author tells a story well, and can describe nature with uncommon power.*"

Bancroft.—THE HISTORY OF THE UNITED STATES OF AMERICA, FROM THE DISCOVERY OF THE CONTINENT. By GEORGE BANCROFT. New and thoroughly Revised Edition. Six Vols. Crown 8vo. 54s.

Barker (Lady).—Works by LADY BARKER :—

A YEAR'S HOUSEKEEPING IN SOUTH AFRICA. With Illustrations. New and Cheaper Edition. Crown 8vo. 6s.

  "*We have to thank Lady Barker for a very amusing book, over which we have spent many a delightful hour, and of which we will not take leave without alluding to the ineffably droll illustrations which add so very much to the enjoyment of her clear and sparkling descriptions.*"—MORNING POST.

Beesly.—STORIES FROM THE HISTORY OF ROME. By Mrs. BEESLY. Extra fcap. 8vo. 2s. 6d.

  "*A little book for which every cultivated and intelligent mother will be grateful for.*"—EXAMINER.

Bismarck—IN THE FRANCO-GERMAN WAR. An Authorized Translation from the German of Dr. MORITZ BUSCH. Two Vols. Crown 8vo. 18s.

  The TIMES *says* :—"*The publication of Bismarck's after-dinner talk, whether discreet or not, will be of priceless biographical value, and Englishmen, at least, will not be disposed to quarrel with Dr. Busch for giving a picture as true to life as Boswell's 'Johnson' of the foremost practical genius that Germany has produced since Frederick the Great.*"

Blackburne.—BIOGRAPHY OF THE RIGHT HON. FRANCIS BLACKBURNE, Late Lord Chancellor of Ireland. Chiefly in connexion with his Public and Political Career. By his Son, EDWARD BLACKBURNE, Q.C. With Portrait Engraved by JEENS. 8vo. 12s.

Blanford (W. T.)—GEOLOGY AND ZOOLOGY OF ABYSSINIA. By W. T. BLANFORD. 8vo. 21s.

Brontë.—CHARLOTTE BRONTË. A Monograph. By T. WEMYSS REID. With Illustrations. Third Edition. Crown 8vo. 6s.

Brooke.—THE RAJA OF SARAWAK: an Account of Sir James Brooke, K.C.B., LL.D. Given chiefly through Letters or Journals. By GERTRUDE L. JACOB. With Portrait and Maps. Two Vols. 8vo. 25s.

Bryce.—Works by JAMES BRYCE, D.C.L., Regius Professor of Civil Law, Oxford :—

THE HOLY ROMAN EMPIRE. Sixth Edition, Revised and Enlarged. Crown 8vo. 7s. 6d.

  "*It exactly supplies a want: it affords a key to much which men read of in their books as isolated facts, but of which they have hitherto had no connected exposition set before them.*"—SATURDAY REVIEW.

Bryce.—*continued.*

TRANSCAUCASIA AND ARARAT: being Notes of a Vacation Tour in the Autumn of 1876. With an Illustration and Map. Third Edition. Crown 8vo. 9s.

"*Mr. Bryce has written a lively and at the same time an instructive description of the tour he made last year in and about the Caucasus. When so well-informed a jurist travels into regions seldom visited, and even walks up a mountain so rarely scaled as Ararat, he is justified in thinking that the impressions he brings home are worthy of being communicated to the world at large, especially when a terrible war is casting a lurid glow over the countries he has lately surveyed.*"—ATHENÆUM.

Burgoyne.—POLITICAL AND MILITARY EPISODES DURING THE FIRST HALF OF THE REIGN OF GEORGE III. Derived from the Life and Correspondence of the Right Hon. J. Burgoyne, Lieut.-General in his Majesty's Army, and M.P. for Preston. By E. B. DE FONBLANQUE. With Portrait, Heliotype Plate, and Maps. 8vo. 16s.

Burke.—EDMUND BURKE, a Historical Study. By JOHN MORLEY, B.A., Oxon. Crown 8vo. 7s. 6d.

Burrows.—WORTHIES OF ALL SOULS: Four Centuries of English History. Illustrated from the College Archives. By MONTAGU BURROWS, Chichele Professor of Modern History at Oxford, Fellow of All Souls. 8vo. 14s.

"*A most amusing as well as a most instructive book.*—GUARDIAN.

Cameron.—OUR FUTURE HIGHWAY. By V. LOVETT CAMERON, C.B., Commander R.N. With Illustrations. 2 vols. Crown 8vo. [*Shortly.*

Campbell.—LOG-LETTERS FROM THE "CHALLENGER." By LORD GEORGE CAMPBELL. With Map. Fifth and cheaper Edition. Crown 8vo. 6s.

"*A delightful book, which we heartily commend to the general reader.*"—SATURDAY REVIEW.

"*We do not hesitate to say that anything so fresh, so picturesque, so generally delightful, as these log-letters has not appeared among books o travel for a long time.*"—EXAMINER.

Campbell.—MY CIRCULAR NOTES: Extracts from Journals; Letters sent Home; Geological and other Notes, written while Travelling Westwards round the World, from July 6th, 1874, to July 6th, 1875. By J. F. CAMPBELL, Author of "Frost and Fire." Cheaper Issue. Crown 8vo. 6s.

Campbell.—TURKS AND GREEKS. Notes of a recent Excursion. By the Hon. DUDLEY CAMPBELL, M.A. With Coloured Map. Crown 8vo. 3s. 6d.

Carpenter.—LIFE AND WORK OF MARY CARPENTER. By the Rev. J. E. CARPENTER. With Portrait engraved by JEENS. Crown 8vo. [*Shortly*.

Carstares.—WILLIAM CARSTARES: a Character and Career of the Revolutionary Epoch (1649—1715). By ROBERT STORY, Minister of Rosneath. 8vo. 12s.

Chatterton: A BIOGRAPHICAL STUDY. By DANIEL WILSON, LL.D., Professor of History and English Literature in University College, Toronto. Crown 8vo. 6s. 6d.

Chatterton: A STORY OF THE YEAR 1770. By Professor MASSON, LL.D. Crown 8vo. 5s.

Clark.—MEMORIALS FROM JOURNALS AND LETTERS OF SAMUEL CLARK, M.A., formerly Principal of the National Society's Training College, Battersea. Edited with Introduction by his WIFE. With Portrait. Crown 8vo. 7s. 6d.

Clifford (W. K.)—LECTURES AND ESSAYS. Edited by LESLIE STEPHEN and FREDERICK POLLOCK, with Introduction by F. POLLOCK. Two Portraits. 2 vols. 8vo. 25s.

The TIMES *of October 22, 1879, says:—"Many a friend of the author on first taking up these volumes and remembering his versatile genius and his keen enjoyment of all realms of intellectual activity must have trembled lest they should be found to consist of fragmentary pieces of work, too disconnected to do justice to his powers of consecutive reasoning and too varied to have any effect as a whole. Fortunately those fears are groundless .... It is not only in subject that the various papers are closely related. There is also a singular consistency of view and of method throughout .... It is in the social and metaphysical subjects that the richness of his intellect shows i'self most forcibly in the variety and originality of the ideas which he presents to us. To appreciate this variety, it is necessary to read the book itself, for it treats, in some form or other, of nearly all the subjects of deepest interest in this age of questioning."*

Combe.—THE LIFE OF GEORGE COMBE, Author of "The Constitution of Man." By CHARLES GIBBON. With Three Portraits engraved by JEENS. Two Vols. 8vo. 32s.

"*A graphic and interesting account of the long life and indefatigable labours of a very remarkable man.*"—SCOTSMAN.

Cooper.—ATHENÆ CANTABRIGIENSES. By CHARLES HENRY COOPER, F.S.A., and THOMPSON COOPER, F.S.A. Vol. I. 8vo., 1500—85, 18s.; Vol. II., 1586—1609, 18s.

Correggio.—ANTONIO ALLEGRI DA CORREGGIO. From the German of Dr. JULIUS MEYER, Director of the Royal Gallery, Berlin. Edited, with an Introduction, by Mrs. HEATON. Containing Twenty Woodbury-type Illustrations. Royal 8vo. Cloth elegant. 31s. 6d.

Cox (G. V.)—RECOLLECTIONS OF OXFORD. By G. V. COX, M.A., New College, late Esquire Bedel and Coroner in the University of Oxford. *Cheaper Edition.* Crown 8vo. 6s.

Cunynghame (Sir A. T.)—MY COMMAND IN SOUTH AFRICA, 1874—78. Comprising Experiences of Travel in the Colonies of South Africa and the Independent States. By Sir ARTHUR THURLOW CUNYNGHAME, G.C.B., then Lieutenant-Governor and Commander of the Forces in South Africa. Third Edition. 8vo. 12s. 6d.

The TIMES *says :—"It is a volume of great interest, ... full of incidents which vividly illustrate the condition of the Colonies and the character and habits of the natives. . . . . It contains valuable illustrations of Cape warfare, and at the present moment it cannot fail to command wide-spread attention."*

"Daily News."—THE DAILY NEWS' CORRESPONDENCE of the War between Germany and France, 1870—1. Edited with Notes and Comments. New Edition. Complete in One Volume. With Maps and Plans. Crown 8vo. 6s.

THE DAILY NEWS' CORRESPONDENCE of the War between Russia and Turkey, to the fall of Kars. Including the letters of Mr. Archibald Forbes, Mr. J. E. McGahan, and other Special Correspondents in Europe and Asia. Second Edition, enlarged. Cheaper Edition. Crown 8vo. 6s.

FROM THE FALL OF KARS TO THE CONCLUSION OF PEACE. Cheaper Edition. Crown 8vo. 6s.

Davidson.—THE LIFE OF A SCOTTISH PROBATIONER; being a Memoir of Thomas Davidson, with his Poems and Letters. By JAMES BROWN, Minister of St. James's Street Church, Paisley. Second Edition, revised and enlarged, with Portrait. Crown 8vo. 7s. 6d.

Deas.—THE RIVER CLYDE. An Historical Description of the Rise and Progress of the Harbour of Glasgow, and of the Improvement of the River from Glasgow to Port Glasgow. By J. DEAS, M. Inst. C.E. 8vo. 10s. 6d.

Denison.—A HISTORY OF CAVALRY FROM THE EARLIEST TIMES. With Lessons for the Future. By Lieut.-Col. GEORGE DENISON, Commanding the Governor-General's Body Guard, Canada, Author of "Modern Cavalry." With Maps and Plans. 8vo. 18s.

Dilke.—GREATER BRITAIN. A Record of Travel in English-speaking Countries during 1866-7. (America, Australia, India. By Sir CHARLES WENTWORTH DILKE, M.P. Sixth Edition. Crown 8vo. 6s.

"*Many of the subjects discussed in these pages,*" *says the* DAILY NEWS, "*are of the widest interest, and such as no man who cares for the future of his race and of the world can afford to treat with indifference.*"

Doyle.—HISTORY OF AMERICA. By J. A. DOYLE. With Maps. 18mo. 4s. 6d.

"*Mr. Doyle's style is clear and simple, his facts are accurately stated, and his book is meritoriously free from prejudice on questions where partisanship runs high amongst us.*"—SATURDAY REVIEW.

Drummond of Hawthornden: THE STORY OF HIS LIFE AND WRITINGS. By PROFESSOR MASSON. With Portrait and Vignette engraved by C. H. JEENS. Crown 8vo. 10s. 6d.

Duff.—Works by M. E. GRANT-DUFF, M.P., late Under Secretary of State for India :—

NOTES OF AN INDIAN JOURNEY. With Map. 8vo. 10s. 6d.

MISCELLANIES POLITICAL AND LITERARY. 8vo. 10s. 6d.

Eadie.—LIFE OF JOHN EADIE, D.D., LL.D. By JAMES BROWN, D.D., Author of "The Life of a Scottish Probationer." With Portrait. Second Edition. Crown 8vo. 7s. 6d.

"*An ably written and characteristic biography.*"—TIMES.

Elliott.—LIFE OF HENRY VENN ELLIOTT, of Brighton. By JOSIAH BATEMAN, M.A. With Portrait, engraved by JEENS. Extra fcap. 8vo. Third and Cheaper Edition. 6s.

Elze.—ESSAYS ON SHAKESPEARE. By Dr. KARL ELZE. Translated with the Author's sanction by L. DORA SCHMITZ. 8vo. 12s.

English Men of Letters. Edited by JOHN MORLEY. A Series of Short Books to tell people what is best worth knowing as to the Life, Character, and Works of some of the great English Writers. In crown 8vo. Price 2s. 6d. each.

English Men of Letters.—*continued.*

I. DR. JOHNSON. By LESLIE STEPHEN.
"*The new series opens well with Mr. Leslie Stephen's sketch of Dr. Johnson. It could hardly have been done better; and it will convey to the readers for whom it is intended a juster estimate of Johnson than either of the two essays of Lord Macaulay*"—PALL MALL GAZETTE.

II. SIR WALTER SCOTT. By R. H. HUTTON.
"*The tone of the volume is excellent throughout.*"—ATHENÆUM.
"*We could not wish for a more suggestive introduction to Scott and his poems and novels.*"—EXAMINER.

III. GIBBON. By J. C. MORISON.
"*As a clear, thoughtful, and attractive record of the life and works of the greatest among the world's historians, it deserves the highest praise.*"—EXAMINER.

IV. SHELLEY. By J. A. SYMONDS.
"*The lovers of this great poet are to be congratulated on having at their command so fresh, clear, and intelligent a presentment of the subject, written by a man of adequate and wide culture.*"—ATHENÆUM.

V. HUME. By Professor HUXLEY.
"*It may fairly be said that no one now living could have expounded Hume with more sympathy or with equal perspicuity.*"—ATHENÆUM.

VI. GOLDSMITH. By WILLIAM BLACK.
"*Mr. Black brings a fine sympathy and taste to bear in his criticism of Goldsmith's writings as well as in his sketch of the incidents of his life.*" ATHENÆUM.

VII. DEFOE. By W. MINTO.
"*Mr. Minto's book is careful and accurate in all that is stated, and faithful in all that it suggests. It will repay reading more than once.*" ATHENÆUM.

VIII. BURNS. By Principal SHAIRP, Professor of Poetry in the University of Oxford.
"*It is impossible to desire fairer criticism than Principal Shairp's on Burns's poetry.... None of the series has given a truer estimate either of character or of genius than this little volume.... and all who read it will be thoroughly grateful to the author for this monument to the genius of Scotland's greatest poet.*"—SPECTATOR.

IX. SPENSER. By the Very Rev. the DEAN OF ST. PAUL'S.
"*Dr. Church is master of his subject, and writes always with good taste.*"—ACADEMY.

X. THACKERAY. By ANTHONY TROLLOPE.
"*Mr. Trollope's sketch is excellently adapted to fulfil the purpose of the series in which it appears.*"—ATHENÆUM.

XI. BURKE. By JOHN MORLEY.
"*Perhaps the best criticism yet published on the life and character of*

English Men of Letters.—*continued.*

Burke is contained in Mr. Morley's compendious biography. His style is vigorous and polished, and both his political and personal judgment, and his literary criticisms are just, generous, subtle, and in a high degree interesting."—SATURDAY REVIEW.

MILTON. By MARK PATTISON. [*Just ready.*]
HAWTHORNE. By HENRY JAMES.
SOUTHEY. By Professor DOWDEN.
CHAUCER. By Professor WARD.
COWPER. By GOLDWIN SMITH. [*In preparation.*]
BUNYAN. By J. A. FROUDE.
WORDSWORTH. By F. W. H. MYERS.

Others in preparation.

Eton College, History of. By H. C. MAXWELL LYTE, M.A.
With numerous Illustrations by Professor DELAMOTTE, Coloured Plates, and a Steel Portrait of the Founder, engraved by C. H. JEENS. New and cheaper Issue, with Corrections. Medium 8vo. Cloth elegant. 21s.

" *We are at length presented with a work on England's greatest public school, worthy of the subject of which it treats. . . . A really valuable and authentic history of Eton College.*"—GUARDIAN.

European History,
Narrated in a Series of Historical Selections from the best Authorities. Edited and arranged by E. M. SEWELL and C. M. YONGE. First Series, crown 8vo. 6s.; Second Series, 1088-1228, crown 8vo. 6s. Third Edition.

" *We know of scarcely anything,*" says the GUARDIAN, *of this volume, "which is so likely to raise to a higher level the average standard of English education.*"

Faraday.—MICHAEL FARADAY.
By J. H. GLADSTONE, Ph.D., F.R.S. Second Edition, with Portrait engraved by JEENS from a photograph by J. WATKINS. Crown 8vo. 4s. 6d.
PORTRAIT. Artist's Proof. 5s.

Forbes.—LIFE AND LETTERS OF JAMES DAVID FORBES,
F.R.S., late Principal of the United College in the University of St. Andrews. By J. C. SHAIRP, LL.D., Principal of the United College in the University of St. Andrews; P. G. TAIT, M.A., Professor of Natural Philosophy in the University of Edinburgh; and A. ADAMS-REILLY, F.R.G.S. 8vo. with Portraits, Map, and Illustrations, 16s.

Freeman.—Works by EDWARD A. FREEMAN, D.C.L., LL.D. :—
HISTORICAL ESSAYS. Third Edition. 8vo. 10s. 6d.
CONTENTS :—*I. " The Mythical and Romantic Elements in Early English History;" II. " The Continuity of English History;" III. " The Relations between the Crowns of England and Scotland;" IV.*

Freeman—*continued.*

"St. Thomas of Canterbury and his Biographers;" V. "The Reign of Edward the Third:" VI. "The Holy Roman Empire;" VII. "The Franks and the Gauls;" VIII. "The Early Sieges of Paris;" IX. "Frederick the First, King of Italy;" X. "The Emperor Frederick the Second:" XI. "Charles the Bold;" XII. "Presidential Government."

HISTORICAL ESSAYS. SECOND SERIES. 8vo. 10s. 6d.

The principal Essays are:—"Ancient Greece and Mediæval Italy:" "Mr. Gladstone's Homer and the Homeric Ages:" "The Historians of Athens:" "The Athenian Democracy:" "Alexander the Great:" "Greece during the Macedonian Period:" "Mommsen's History of Rome:" "Lucius Cornelius Sulla:" "The Flavian Cæsars."

HISTORICAL ESSAYS. Third Series. 8vo. 12s.

CONTENTS:—"First Impressions of Rome." "The Illyrian Emperors and their Land." "Augusta Treverorum." "The Goths at Ravenna." "Race and Language." "The Byzantine Empire." "First Impressions of Athens." "Mediæval and Modern Greece." "The Southern Slaves." "Sicilian Cycles." "The Normans at Palermo."

COMPARATIVE POLITICS.—Lectures at the Royal Institution. To which is added the "Unity of History," the Rede Lecture at Cambridge, 1872. 8vo. 14s.

THE HISTORY AND CONQUESTS OF THE SARACENS. Six Lectures. Third Edition, with New Preface. Crown 8vo. 3s. 6d.

HISTORICAL AND ARCHITECTURAL SKETCHES: chiefly Italian. With Illustrations by the Author. Crown 8vo. 10s. 6d.

HISTORY OF FEDERAL GOVERNMENT, from the Foundation of the Achaian League to the Disruption of the United States. Vol. I. General Introduction. History of the Greek Federations. 8vo. 21s.

OLD ENGLISH HISTORY. With *Five Coloured Maps.* Fourth Edition. Extra fcap. 8vo., half-bound. 6s.

"*The book indeed is full of instruction and interest to students of all ages, and he must be a well-informed man indeed who will not rise from its perusal with clearer and more accurate ideas of a too much neglected portion of English history.*"—SPECTATOR.

HISTORY OF THE CATHEDRAL CHURCH OF WELLS, as illustrating the History of the Cathedral Churches of the Old Foundation. Crown 8vo. 3s. 6d.

"*The history assumes in Mr. Freeman's hands a significance, and, we may add, a practical value as suggestive of what a cathedral ought to be, which make it well worthy of mention.*"—SPECTATOR.

Freeman—*continued.*
> THE GROWTH OF THE ENGLISH CONSTITUTION FROM THE EARLIEST TIMES. Crown 8vo. 5s. Third Edition, revised.
>
> GENERAL SKETCH OF EUROPEAN HISTORY. Being Vol. I. of a Historical Course for Schools edited by E. A. FREEMAN. New Edition, enlarged with Maps, Chronological Table, Index, &c. 18mo. 3s. 6d.
>
> "*It supplies the great want of a good foundation for historical teaching. The scheme is an excellent one, and this instalment has been accepted in a way that promises much for the volumes that are yet to appear.*"—EDUCATIONAL TIMES.
>
> THE OTTOMAN POWER IN EUROPE: its Nature, its Growth, and its Decline. With Three Coloured Maps. Crown 8vo. 7s. 6d.

Galileo.—THE PRIVATE LIFE OF GALILEO. Compiled principally from his Correspondence and that of his eldest daughter, Sister Maria Celeste, Nun in the Franciscan Convent of S. Matthew in Arcetri. With Portrait. Crown 8vo. 7s. 6d.

Geddes.—THE PROBLEM OF THE HOMERIC POEMS. By W. D. GEDDES, LL.D., Professor of Greek in the University of Aberdeen. 8vo. 14s.

Gladstone—Works by the Right Hon. W. E. GLADSTONE, M.P.:—
> JUVENTUS MUNDI. The Gods and Men of the Heroic Age. Crown 8vo. cloth. With Map. 10s. 6d. Second Edition.
>
> "*Seldom,*" says the ATHENÆUM, "*out of the great poems themselves, have these Divinities looked so majestic and respectable. To read these brilliant details is like standing on the Olympian threshold and gazing at the ineffable brightness within.*"
>
> HOMERIC SYNCHRONISM. An inquiry into the Time and Place of Homer. Crown 8vo. 6s.
>
> "*It is impossible not to admire the immense range of thought and inquiry which the author has displayed.*"—BRITISH QUARTERLY REVIEW.

Goethe and Mendelssohn (1821—1831). Translated from the German of Dr. KARL MENDELSSOHN, Son of the Composer, by M. E. VON GLEHN. From the Private Diaries and Home Letters of Mendelssohn, with Poems and Letters of Goethe never before printed. Also with two New and Original Portraits, Facsimiles, and Appendix of Twenty Letters hitherto unpublished. Crown 8vo. 5s. Second Edition, enlarged.

"... Every page is full of interest, not merely to the musician, but to the general reader. The book is a very charming one, on a topic of deep and lasting interest."—STANDARD.

Goldsmid.—TELEGRAPH AND TRAVEL. A Narrative of the Formation and Development of Telegraphic Communication between England and India, under the orders of Her Majesty's Government, with incidental Notices of the Countries traversed by the Lines. By Colonel Sir FREDERIC GOLDSMID, C.B., K.C.S.I., late Director of the Government Indo-European Telegraph. With numerous Illustrations and Maps. 8vo. 21s.

"The merit of the work is a total absence of exaggeration, which does not, however, preclude a vividness and vigour of style not always characteristic of similar narratives."—STANDARD.

Gordon.—LAST LETTERS FROM EGYPT, to which are added Letters from the Cape. By LADY DUFF GORDON. With a Memoir by her Daughter, Mrs. Ross, and Portrait engraved by JEENS. Second Edition. Crown 8vo. 9s.

"The intending tourist who wishes to acquaint himself with the country he is about to visit, stands embarrassed amidst the riches presented for his choice, and in the end probably rests contented with the sober usefulness of Murray. He will not, however, if he is well advised, grudge a place in his portmanteau to this book."—TIMES.

Gray.—CHINA. A History of the Laws, Manners, and Customs of the People. By the VENERABLE JOHN HENRY GRAY, LL.D., Archdeacon of Hong Kong, formerly H.B.M. Consular Chaplain at Canton. Edited by W. Gow Gregor. With 150 Full-page Illustrations, being Facsimiles of Drawings by a Chinese Artist. 2 Vols. Demy 8vo. 32s.

"Its pages contain the most truthful and vivid picture of Chinese life which has ever been published."—ATHENÆUM.

"The only elaborate and valuable book we have had for many years treating generally of the people of the Celestial Empire."—ACADEMY.

Green.—Works by JOHN RICHARD GREEN :—

HISTORY OF THE ENGLISH PEOPLE. Vol. I.—Early England—Foreign Kings—The Charter—The Parliament. With 8 Coloured Maps. 8vo. 16s. Vol. II.—The Monarchy, 1461—1540; the Restoration, 1540—1603. 8vo. 16s. Vol. III. —Puritan England, 1603—1660; the Revolution, 1660—1688. With 4 Maps. 8vo. 16s. [Vol. IV. in the press.

"Mr. Green has done a work which probably no one but himself could have done. He has read and assimilated the results of all the labours of students during the last half century in the field of English history, and has given them a fresh meaning by his own independent study. He has fused together by the force of sympathetic imagination all that he has so

Green.—*continued.*

collected, and has given us a vivid and forcible sketch of the march of English history. His book, both in its aims and its accomplishments, rises far beyond any of a similar kind, and it will give the colouring to the popular view to English history for some time to come."—EXAMINER.

A SHORT HISTORY OF THE ENGLISH PEOPLE. With Coloured Maps, Genealogical Tables, and Chronological Annals. Crown 8vo. 8s. 6d. Sixty-third Thousand.

"To say that Mr. Green's book is better than those which have preceded it, would be to convey a very inadequate impression of its merits. It stands alone as the one general history of the country, for the sake of which all others, if young and old are wise, will be speedily and surely set aside."

STRAY STUDIES FROM ENGLAND AND ITALY. Crown 8vo. 8s. 6d. Containing : Lambeth and the Archbishops—The Florence of Dante—Venice and Rome—Early History of Oxford—The District Visitor—Capri—Hotels in the Clouds—Sketches in Sunshine, &c.

"One and all of the papers are eminently readable."—ATHENÆUM.

Guest.—LECTURES ON THE HISTORY OF ENGLAND. By M. J. GUEST. With Maps. Crown 8vo. 6s.

"The book is pleasant reading, it is full of information, much of it is valuable, most of it is correct, told in a gossipy and intelligible way."—ATHENÆUM.

Hamerton.—Works by P. G. HAMERTON :—

THE INTELLECTUAL LIFE. With a Portrait of Leonardo da Vinci, etched by LEOPOLD FLAMENG. Second Edition. Crown 10s. 6d. 8vo.

"We have read the whole book with great pleasure, and we can recommend it strongly to all who can appreciate grave reflections on a very important subject, excellently illustrated from the resources of a mind stored with much reading and much keen observation of real life."—SATURDAY REVIEW.

THOUGHTS ABOUT ART. New Edition, revised, with an Introduction. Crown 8vo. 8s. 6d.

"A manual of sound and thorough criticism on art."—STANDARD.

Hill.—THE RECORDER OF BIRMINGHAM. A Memoir of Matthew Davenport Hill, with Selections from his Correspondence. By his Daughters ROSAMOND and FLORENCE DAVENPORT-HILL. With Portrait engraved by C. H. JEENS. 8vo. 16s.

Hill.—WHAT WE SAW IN AUSTRALIA. By ROSAMOND and FLORENCE HILL. Crown 8vo. 10s. 6d.

"*May be recommended as an interesting and truthful picture of the condition of those lands which are so distant and yet so much like home.*"—SATURDAY REVIEW.

Hodgson.—MEMOIR OF REV. FRANCIS HODGSON, B.D., Scholar, Poet, and Divine. By his Son, the Rev. JAMES T. HODGSON, M.A. Containing numerous Letters from Lord Byron and others. With Portrait engraved by JEENS. Two Vols. Crown 8vo. 18s.

"*A book that has added so much of a healthy nature to our knowledge of Byron, and that contains so rich a store of delightful correspondence.*"—ATHENÆUM.

Hole.—A GENEALOGICAL STEMMA OF THE KINGS OF ENGLAND AND FRANCE. By the Rev. C. HOLE, M.A., Trinity College, Cambridge. On Sheet, 1s.

A BRIEF BIOGRAPHICAL DICTIONARY. Compiled and Arranged by the Rev. CHARLES HOLE, M.A. Second Edition. 18mo. 4s. 6d.

Hooker and Ball.—MAROCCO AND THE GREAT ATLAS: Journal of a Tour in. By Sir JOSEPH D. HOOKER, K.C.S.I., C.B., F.R.S., &c., and JOHN BALL, F.R.S. With an Appendix, including a Sketch of the Geology of Marocco, by G. MAW, F.L.S., F.G.S. With Illustrations and Map. 8vo. 21s.

"*It is long since any more interesting book of travels has issued from our press.*"—SATURDAY REVIEW. "*This is, without doubt, one of the most interesting and valuable books of travel published for many years.*"—SPECTATOR.

Hozier (H. M.)—Works by CAPTAIN HENRY M. HOZIER, late Assistant Military Secretary to Lord Napier of Magdala :—

THE SEVEN WEEKS' WAR; Its Antecedents and Incidents. *New and Cheaper Edition.* With New Preface, Maps, and Plans. Crown 8vo. 6s.

THE INVASIONS OF ENGLAND: a History of the Past, with Lessons for the Future. Two Vols. 8vo. 28s.

Hübner.—A RAMBLE ROUND THE WORLD IN 1871. By M. LE BARON HÜBNER, formerly Ambassador and Minister. Translated by LADY HERBERT. New and Cheaper Edition. With numerous Illustrations. Crown 8vo. 6s.

"*It is difficult to do ample justice to this pleasant narrative of travel .... it does not contain a single dull paragraph.*"—MORNING POST.

Hughes.—Works by THOMAS HUGHES, Q.C., Author of "Tom Brown's School Days."
ALFRED THE GREAT. New Edition. Crown 8vo. 6s.
MEMOIR OF A BROTHER. With Portrait of GEORGE HUGHES, after WATTS. Engraved by JEENS. Crown 8vo. 5s. Sixth Edition.
"*The boy who can read this book without deriving from it some additional impulse towards honourable, manly, and independent conduct, has no good stuff in him*"—DAILY NEWS.

Hunt.—HISTORY OF ITALY. By the Rev. W. HUNT, M.A. Being the Fourth Volume of the Historical Course for Schools. Edited by EDWARD A. FREEMAN, D.C.L. 18mo. 3s.
"*Mr. Hunt gives us a most compact but very readable little book, containing in small compass a very complete outline of a complicated and perplexing subject. It is a book which may be safely recommended to others besides schoolboys.*"—JOHN BULL.

Irving.—THE ANNALS OF OUR TIME. A Diurnal of Events, Social and Political, Home and Foreign, from the Accession of Queen Victoria to the Peace of Versailles. By JOSEPH IRVING. *Fourth Edition.* 8vo. half-bound. 16s.
ANNALS OF OUR TIME. Supplement. From Feb. 28, 1871, to March 19, 1874. 8vo. 4s. 6d.
ANNALS OF OUR TIME. Second Supplement. From March, 1874, to the Occupation of Cyprus. 8vo. 4s. 6d.
"*We have before us a trusty and ready guide to the events of the past thirty years, available equally for the statesman, the politician, the public writer, and the general reader.*"—TIMES.

James.—Works by HENRY JAMES, Jun. FRENCH POETS AND NOVELISTS. Crown 8vo. 8s. 6d.
CONTENTS:—*Alfred de Musset; Théophile Gautier; Baudelaire; Honoré de Balzac; George Sand; The Two Ampères; Turgenieff, &c.*

Johnson's Lives of the Poets.—The Six Chief Lives—Milton, Dryden, Swift, Addison, Pope, Gray. With Macaulay's "Life of Johnson." Edited, with Preface, by MATTHEW ARNOLD. Crown 8vo. 6s.

Killen.—ECCLESIASTICAL HISTORY OF IRELAND, from the Earliest Date to the Present Time. By W. D. KILLEN, D.D., President of Assembly's College, Belfast, and Professor of Ecclesiastical History. Two Vols. 8vo. 25s.
"*Those who have the leisure will do well to read these two volumes. They are full of interest, and are the result of great research.... We*

have no hesitation in recommending the work to all who wish to improve their acquaintance with Irish history."—SPECTATOR.

Kingsley (Charles).—Works by the Rev. CHARLES KINGSLEY, M.A., Rector of Eversley and Canon of Westminster. (For other Works by the same Author, see THEOLOGICAL and BELLES LETTRES Catalogues.)

ON THE ANCIEN RÉGIME as it existed on the Continent before the FRENCH REVOLUTION. Three Lectures delivered at the Royal Institution. Crown 8vo. 6s.

AT LAST: A CHRISTMAS in the WEST INDIES. With nearly Fifty Illustrations. Sixth Edition. Crown 8vo. 6s.

*Mr. Kingsley's dream of forty years was at last fulfilled, when he started on a Christmas expedition to the West Indies, for the purpose of becoming personally acquainted with the scenes which he has so vividly described in "Westward Ho!" These two volumes are the journal of his voyage. Records of natural history, sketches of tropical landscape, chapters on education, views of society, all find their place. "We can only say that Mr. Kingsley's account of a 'Christmas in the West Indies' is in every way worthy to be classed among his happiest productions."—*STANDARD.

THE ROMAN AND THE TEUTON. A Series of Lectures delivered before the University of Cambridge. New and Cheaper Edition, with Preface by Professor MAX MÜLLER. Crown 8vo. 6s.

PLAYS AND PURITANS, and other Historical Essays. With Portrait of Sir WALTER RALEIGH. New Edition. Crown 8vo. 6s.

In addition to the Essay mentioned in the title, this volume contains other two—one on "Sir Walter Raleigh and his Time," and one on Froude's "History of England."

Kingsley (Henry).—TALES OF OLD TRAVEL. Re-narrated by HENRY KINGSLEY, F.R.G.S. With *Eight Illustrations* by HUARD. Fifth Edition. Crown 8vo. 5s.

"*We know no better book for those who want knowledge or seek to refresh it. As for the 'sensational,' most novels are tame compared with these narratives.*"—ATHENÆUM.

Lang.—CYPRUS: Its History, its Present Resources and Future Prospects. By R. HAMILTON LANG, late H.M. Consul for the Island of Cyprus. With Two Illustrations and Four Maps. 8vo. 14s.

"*The fair and impartial account of her past and present to be found in these pages has an undoubted claim on the attention of all intelligent readers.*"—MORNING POST.

Laocoon.—Translated from the Text of Lessing, with Preface and Notes by the Right Hon. SIR ROBERT J. PHILLIMORE, D.C.L. With Photographs. 8vo. 12s.

Leonardo da Vinci and his Works.—Consisting of a Life of Leonardo Da Vinci, by MRS. CHARLES W. HEATON, Author of "Albrecht Dürer of Nürnberg," &c., an Essay on his Scientific and Literary Works by CHARLES CHRISTOPHER BLACK, M.A., and an account of his more important Paintings and Drawings. Illustrated with Permanent Photographs. Royal 8vo, cloth, extra gilt. 31s. 6d.

Liechtenstein.—HOLLAND HOUSE. By Princess MARIE LIECHTENSTEIN. With Five Steel Engravings by C. H. JEENS, after Paintings by WATTS and other celebrated Artists, and numerous Illustrations drawn by Professor P. H. DELAMOTTE, and engraved on Wood by J. D. COOPER, W. PALMER, and JEWITT & Co. Third and Cheaper Edition. Medium 8vo. cloth elegant. 16s.

Also, an Edition containing, in addition to the above, about 40 Illustrations by the Woodbury-type process, and India Proofs of the Steel Engravings. Two vols. medium 4to. half morocco elegant. 4l. 4s.

Lloyd.—THE AGE OF PERICLES. A History of the Arts and Politics of Greece from the Persian to the Peloponnesian War. By W. WATKISS LLOYD. Two Vols. 8vo. 21s.

"*No such account of Greek art of the best period has yet been brought together in an English work. . . . . Mr. Lloyd has produced a book of unusual excellence and interest.*"—PALL MALL GAZETTE.

Loch Etive and the Sons of Uisnach.—With Illustrations. 8vo. 14s.

"*Not only have we Loch Etive of the present time brought before us in colours as true as they are vivid, but stirring scenes which happened on the borders of the beautiful lake in semi-mythical times are conjured up with singular skill. Nowhere else do we remember to have met with such a well-written account of the invasion of Scotland by the Irish.*"—GLOBE.

Loftie.—A RIDE IN EGYPT FROM SIOOT TO LUXOR, IN 1879; with Notes on the Present State and Ancient History of the Nile Valley, and some account of the various ways of making the voyage out and home. By the Rev. W. J. LOFTIE. With Illustrations. Crown 8vo. 10s. 6d.

"*We prophesy that Mr. Loftie's little book will accompany many travellers on the Nile in the coming winters.*"—TIMES.

Lubbock.—ADDRESSES, POLITICAL AND EDUCATIONAL. By Sir JOHN LUBBOCK, Bart., M.P., D.C.L., F.R.S. 8vo. 8s. 6d.

Macdonell.—FRANCE SINCE THE FIRST EMPIRE. By JAMES MACDONELL. Edited with Preface by his Wife. Crown 8vo. [*Shortly.*

Macarthur.—HISTORY OF SCOTLAND, By MARGARET MACARTHUR. Being the Third Volume of the Historical Course for Schools, Edited by EDWARD A. FREEMAN, D.C.L. Second Edition. 18mo. 2s.

"*It is an excellent summary, unimpeachable as to facts, and putting them in the clearest and most impartial light attainable.*"—GUARDIAN.
"*No previous History of Scotland of the same bulk is anything like so trustworthy, or deserves to be so extensively used as a text-book.*"—GLOBE.

Macmillan (Rev. Hugh).—For other Works by same Author, see THEOLOGICAL and SCIENTIFIC CATALOGUES.

HOLIDAYS ON HIGH LANDS; or, Rambles and Incidents in search of Alpine Plants. Second Edition, revised and enlarged. Globe 8vo. cloth. 6s.

"*Botanical knowledge is blended with a love of nature, a pious enthusiasm, and a rich felicity of diction not to be met with in any works of kindred character, if we except those of Hugh Miller.*"—TELEGRAPH.

Macready.—MACREADY'S REMINISCENCES AND SELECTIONS FROM HIS DIARIES AND LETTERS. Edited by Sir F. POLLOCK, Bart., one of his Executors. With Four Portraits engraved by JEENS. New and Cheaper Edition. Crown 8vo. 7s. 6d.

"*As a careful and for the most part just estimate of the stage during a very brilliant period, the attraction of these volumes can scarcely be surpassed. . . . . Readers who have no special interest in theatrical matters, but enjoy miscellaneous gossip, will be allured from page to page, attracted by familiar names and by observations upon popular actors and authors.*"—SPECTATOR.

Mahaffy.—Works by the Rev. J. P. MAHAFFY, M.A., Fellow of Trinity College, Dublin:—

SOCIAL LIFE IN GREECE FROM HOMER TO MENANDER. Third Edition, revised and enlarged, with a new chapter on Greek Art. Crown 8vo. 9s.

"*It should be in the hands of all who desire thoroughly to understand and to enjoy Greek literature, and to get an intelligent idea of the old Greek life, political, social, and religious.*"—GUARDIAN.

HISTORY, BIOGRAPHY, TRAVELS, ETC.

Mahaffy.—*continued.*
RAMBLES AND STUDIES IN GREECE. With Illustrations. Crown 8vo. 10s. 6d. New and enlarged Edition, with Map and Illustrations.
"*A singularly instructive and agreeable volume.*"—ATHENÆUM.

"Maori."—SPORT AND WORK ON THE NEPAUL FRONTIER; or, Twelve Years' Sporting Reminiscences of an Indigo Planter. By "MAORI." With Illustrations. 8vo. 14s.
"*Every day's adventures, with all the joys and perils of the chase, are told as only a keen and cunning sportsman can tell them.*"—STANDARD.

Margary.—THE JOURNEY OF AUGUSTUS RAYMOND MARGARY FROM SHANGHAE TO BHAMO AND BACK TO MANWYNE. From his Journals and Letters, with a brief Biographical Preface, a concluding chapter by Sir RUTHERFORD ALCOCK, K.C.B., and a Steel Portrait engraved by JEENS, and Map. 8vo. 10s. 6d.
"*There is a manliness, a cheerful spirit, an inherent vigour which was never overcome by sickness or debility, a tact which conquered the prejudices of a strange and suspicious population, a quiet self-reliance, always combined with deep religious feeling, unalloyed by either priggishness, cant, or superstition, that ought to commend this volume to readers sitting quietly at home who feel any pride in the high estimation accorded to men of their race at Yarkand or at Khiva, in the heart of Africa, or on the shores of Lake Seri-kul.*"—SATURDAY REVIEW.

Markham.—NORTHWARD HO! By Captain ALBERT H. MARKHAM, R.N., Author of "The Great Frozen Sea," &c. Including a Narrative of Captain Phipps's Expedition, by a Midshipman. With Illustrations. Crown 8vo. 10s. 6d.
"*Captain Markham's interesting volume has the advantage of being written by a man who is practically conversant with the subject.*"—PALL MALL GAZETTE.

Martin.—THE HISTORY OF LLOYD'S, AND OF MARINE INSURANCE IN GREAT BRITAIN. With an Appendix containing Statistics relating to Marine Insurance. By FREDERICK MARTIN, Author of "The Statesman's Year Book." 8vo. 14s.

Martineau.—BIOGRAPHICAL SKETCHES, 1852—1875. By HARRIET MARTINEAU. With Additional Sketches, and Autobiographical Sketch. Fifth Edition. Crown 8vo. 6s.

Masson (David).—For other Works by same Author, *see* PHILOSOPHICAL and BELLES LETTRES CATALOGUES.

Masson (David).—*continued.*

CHATTERTON: A Story of the Year 1770. By DAVID MASSON, LL.D., Professor of Rhetoric and English Literature in the University of Edinburgh. Crown 8vo. 5s.

THE THREE DEVILS: Luther's, Goethe's, and Milton's; and other Essays. Crown 8vo. 5s.

WORDSWORTH, SHELLEY, AND KEATS; and other Essays. Crown 8vo. 5s.

Mathews.—LIFE OF CHARLES J. MATHEWS, Chiefly Autobiographical. With Selections from his Correspondence and Speeches. Edited by CHARLES DICKENS.

"*One of the pleasantest and most readable books of the season. From first to last these two volumes are alive with the inimitable artist and comedian. . . . The whole book is full of life, vigour, and wit, and even through some of the gloomy episodes of volume two, will repay most careful study. So complete, so varied a picture of a man's life is rarely to be met with.*"—STANDARD.

Maurice.—THE FRIENDSHIP OF BOOKS; AND OTHER LECTURES. By the REV. F. D. MAURICE. Edited with Preface, by THOMAS HUGHES, Q.C. Crown 8vo. 10s. 6d.

Mayor (J. E. B.)—WORKS edited by JOHN E. B. MAYOR, M.A., Kennedy Professor of Latin at Cambridge:—

CAMBRIDGE IN THE SEVENTEENTH CENTURY. Part II. Autobiography of Matthew Robinson. Fcap. 8vo. 5s. 6d.

LIFE OF BISHOP BEDELL. By his SON. Fcap. 8vo. 3s. 6d.

Melbourne.—MEMOIRS OF THE RT. HON. WILLIAM, SECOND VISCOUNT MELBOURNE. By W. M. TORRENS, M.P. With Portrait after Sir. T. Lawrence. Second Edition. 2 Vols. 8vo. 32s.

"*As might be expected, he has produced a book which will command and reward attention. It contains a great deal of valuable matter and a great deal of animated, elegant writing.*"—QUARTERLY REVIEW.

Mendelssohn.—LETTERS AND RECOLLECTIONS. By FERDINAND HILLER. Translated by M. E. VON GLEHN. With Portrait from a Drawing by KARL MÜLLER, never before published. Second Edition. Crown 8vo. 7s. 6d.

"*This is a very interesting addition to our knowledge of the great German composer. It reveals him to us under a new light, as the warm-hearted comrade, the musician whose soul was in his work, and the home-loving, domestic man.*"—STANDARD.

HISTORY, BIOGRAPHY, TRAVELS, ETC. 21

Merewether.—BY SEA AND BY LAND. Being a Trip through Egypt, India, Ceylon, Australia, New Zealand, and America—all Round the World. By HENRY ALWORTH MEREWETHER, one of Her Majesty's Counsel. Crown 8vo. 8s. 6d.

Michael Angelo Buonarotti; Sculptor, Painter, Architect. The Story of his Life and Labours. By C. C. BLACK, M.A. Illustrated by 20 Permanent Photographs. Royal 8vo. cloth elegant, 31s. 6d.

"*The story of Michael Angelo's life remains interesting whatever be the manner of telling it, and supported as it is by this beautiful series of photographs, the volume must take rank among the most splendid of Christmas books, fitted to serve and to outlive the season.*"—PALL MALL GAZETTE.

Michelet.—A SUMMARY OF MODERN HISTORY. Translated from the French of M. MICHELET, and continued to the present time by M. C. M. SIMPSON. Globe 8vo. 4s. 6d.

Milton.—LIFE OF JOHN MILTON. Narrated in connection with the Political, Ecclesiastical, and Literary History of his Time. By DAVID MASSON, M.A., LL.D., Professor of Rhetoric and English Literature in the University of Edinburgh. With Portraits. Vol. I. 18s. Vol. II., 1638—1643. 8vo. 16s. Vol. III. 1643—1649. 8vo. 18s. Vols. IV. and V. 1649—1660. 32s. Vol. VI. concluding the work in the press.

This work is not only a Biography, but also a continuous Political, Ecclesiastical, and Literary History of England through Milton's whole time.

Mitford (A. B.)—TALES OF OLD JAPAN. By A. B. MITFORD, Second Secretary to the British Legation in Japan. With upwards of 30 Illustrations, drawn and cut on Wood by Japanese Artists. New and Cheaper Edition. Crown 8vo. 6s.

"*These very original volumes will always be interesting as memorials of a most exceptional society, while regarded simply as tales, they are sparkling, sensational, and dramatic.*"—PALL MALL GAZETTE.

Monteiro.—ANGOLA AND THE RIVER CONGO. By JOACHIM MONTEIRO. With numerous Illustrations from Sketches taken on the spot, and a Map. Two Vols. crown 8vo. 21s.

Morison.—THE LIFE AND TIMES OF SAINT BERNARD, Abbot of Clairvaux. By JAMES COTTER MORISON, M.A. New Edition. Crown 8vo. 6s.

Moseley.—NOTES BY A NATURALIST ON THE *CHALLENGER*: being an Account of various Observations made during the Voyage of H.M.S. *Challenger*, Round the World, in 1872–76. By H. N. MOSELEY, F.R.S., Member of the Scientific Staff of the *Challenger*. 8vo. with Maps, Coloured Plates, and Woodcuts. 21*s*.

"*This is certainly the most interesting and suggestive book, descriptive of a naturalist's travels, which has been published since Mr. Darwin's 'Journal of Researches' appeared, more than forty years ago.*"—NATURE. "*We cannot point to any book of travels in our day more vivid in its powers of description, more varied in its subject matter, or more attractive to every educated reader.*"—SATURDAY REVIEW.

Murray.—ROUND ABOUT FRANCE. By E. C. GRENVILLE MURRAY. Crown 8vo. 7*s*. 6*d*.

"*These short essays are a perfect mine of information as to the present condition and future prospects of political parties in France. . . . It is at once extremely interesting and exceptionally instructive on a subject on which few English people are well informed.*"—SCOTSMAN.

Napier.—MACVEY NAPIER'S SELECTED CORRESPONDENCE. Edited by his Son, MACVEY NAPIER. 8vo. 14*s*.

The TIMES *says* :—"*It is replete with useful material for the biographers of many distinguished writers of the generation which is passing away. Since reading it we understand several noteworthy men, and Brougham in particular, far better than we did before.*" "*It would be useless to attempt within our present limits to give any adequate idea of the abundance of interesting passages which meet us in the letters of Macaulay, Brougham, Carlyle, Jeffrey, Senior, and many other well-known writers. Especially piquant are Jeffrey's periodical criticisms on the contents of the Review which he had formerly edited.*"—PALL MALL GAZETTE.

Napoleon.—THE HISTORY OF NAPOLEON I. By P. LANFREY. A Translation with the sanction of the Author. 4 vols. 8vo. Vols. I. II. and III. price 12*s*. each. Vol. IV. 6*s*.

The PALL MALL GAZETTE *says it is* "*one of the most striking pieces of historical composition of which France has to boast,*" *and the* SATURDAY REVIEW *calls it* "*an excellent translation of a work on every ground deserving to be translated. It is unquestionably and immeasurably the best that has been produced. It is in fact the only work to which we can turn for an accurate and trustworthy narrative of that extraordinary career. . . . The book is the best and indeed the only trustworthy history of Napoleon which has been written.*"

Nichol.—TABLES OF EUROPEAN LITERATURE AND HISTORY, A.D. 200—1876. By J. NICHOL, LL.D., Professor of English Language and Literature, Glasgow. 4to. 6*s*. 6*d*.

TABLES OF ANCIENT LITERATURE AND HISTORY, B.C. 1500—A.D. 200. By the same Author. 4to. 4*s*. 6*d*.

HISTORY, BIOGRAPHY, TRAVELS, ETC. 23

Nordenskiöld's Arctic Voyages, 1858-79. — With Maps and numerous Illustrations. 8vo. 16s.

"*A volume of great interest and much scientific value.*"—NATURE.

Oliphant (Mrs.).—THE MAKERS OF FLORENCE: Dante Giotto, Savonarola, and their City. By Mrs. OLIPHANT. With numerous Illustrations from drawings by Professor DELAMOTTE, and portrait of Savonarola, engraved by JEENS. Second Edition. Medium 8vo. Cloth extra. 21s.

"*We are grateful to Mrs. Oliphant for her eloquent and beautiful sketches of Dante, Fra Angelico, and Savonarola. They are picturesque, full of life, and rich in detail, and they are charmingly illustrated by the art of the engraver.*"—SPECTATOR.

Oliphant.—THE DUKE AND THE SCHOLAR; and other Essays. By T. L. KINGTON OLIPHANT. 8vo. 7s. 6d.

"*This volume contains one of the most beautiful biographical essays we have seen since Macaulay's days.*"—STANDARD.

Otte.—SCANDINAVIAN HISTORY. By E. C. OTTE. With Maps. Extra fcap. 8vo. 6s.

Owens College Essays and Addresses.—By PROFESSORS AND LECTURERS OF OWENS COLLEGE, MANCHESTER. Published in Commemoration of the Opening of the New College Buildings, October 7th, 1873. 8vo. 14s.

Palgrave (R. F. D.)—THE HOUSE OF COMMONS; Illustrations of its History and Practice. By REGINALD F. D. PALGRAVE, Clerk Assistant of the House of Commons. New and Revised Edition. Crown 8vo. 2s. 6d.

Palgrave (Sir F.)—HISTORY OF NORMANDY AND OF ENGLAND. By Sir FRANCIS PALGRAVE, Deputy Keeper of Her Majesty's Public Records. Completing the History to the Death of William Rufus. 4 Vols. 8vo. 4l. 4s.

Palgrave (W. G.)—A NARRATIVE OF A YEAR'S JOURNEY THROUGH CENTRAL AND EASTERN ARABIA, 1862-3. By WILLIAM GIFFORD PALGRAVE, late of the Eighth Regiment Bombay N. I. Sixth Edition. With Maps, Plans, and Portrait of Author, engraved on steel by Jeens. Crown 8vo. 6s.

"*He has not only written one of the best books on the Arabs and one of the best books on Arabia, but he has done so in a manner that must command the respect no less than the admiration of his fellow-countrymen.*"—FORTNIGHTLY REVIEW.

Palgrave.—*continued.*
ESSAYS ON EASTERN QUESTIONS. By W. GIFFORD PALGRAVE. 8vo. 10s. 6d.

"*These essays are full of anecdote and interest. The book is decidedly a valuable addition to the stock of literature on which men must base their opinion of the difficult social and political problems suggested by the designs of Russia, the capacity of Mahometans for sovereignty, and the good government and retention of India.*"—SATURDAY REVIEW.

DUTCH GUIANA. With Maps and Plans. 8vo. 9s.

"*His pages are nearly exhaustive as far as facts and statistics go, while they are lightened by graphic social sketches as well as sparkling descriptions of scenery.*"—SATURDAY REVIEW.

Patteson.—LIFE AND LETTERS OF JOHN COLERIDGE PATTESON, D.D., Missionary Bishop of the Melanesian Islands. By CHARLOTTE M. YONGE, Author of "The Heir of Redclyffe." With Portraits after RICHMOND and from Photograph, engraved by JEENS. With Map. Fifth Edition. Two Vols. Crown 8vo. 12s.

"*Miss Yonge's work is in one respect a model biography. It is made up almost entirely of Patteson's own letters. Aware that he had left his home once and for all, his correspondence took the form of a diary, and as we read on we come to know the man, and to love him almost as if we had seen him.*"—ATHENÆUM. "*Such a life, with its grand lessons of unselfishness, is a blessing and an honour to the age in which it is lived; the biography cannot be studied without pleasure and profit, and indeed we should think little of the man who did not rise from the study of it better and wiser. Neither the Church nor the nation which produces such sons need ever despair of its future.*"—SATURDAY REVIEW.

Pauli.—PICTURES OF OLD ENGLAND. By Dr. REINHOLD PAULI. Translated, with the approval of the Author, by E. C. OTTÉ. Cheaper Edition. Crown 8vo. 6s.

Payne.—A HISTORY OF EUROPEAN COLONIES. By E. J. PAYNE, M.A. With Maps. 18mo. 4s. 6d.

The TIMES says:—"*We have seldom met with a historian capable of forming a more comprehensive, far-seeing, and unprejudiced estimate of events and peoples, and we can commend this little work as one certain to prove of the highest interest to all thoughtful readers.*"

Persia.—EASTERN PERSIA. An Account of the Journeys of the Persian Boundary Commission, 1870-1-2.—Vol. I. The Geography, with Narratives by Majors ST. JOHN, LOVETT, and EUAN SMITH, and an Introduction by Major-General Sir FREDERIC GOLDSMID, C.B., K.C.S.I., British Commissioner and Arbitrator.

HISTORY, BIOGRAPHY, TRAVELS, ETC. 25

With Maps and Illustrations.—Vol. II. The Zoology and Geology. By W. T. BLANFORD, A.R.S.M., F.R.S. With Coloured Illustrations. Two Vols. 8vo. 42s.

"*The volumes largely increase our store of information about countries with which Englishmen ought to be familiar. . . . . They throw into the shade all that hitherto has appeared in our tongue respecting the local features of Persia, its scenery, its resources, even its social condition. They contain also abundant evidence of English endurance, daring, and spirit.*"—TIMES.

Prichard.—THE ADMINISTRATION OF INDIA. From 1859 to 1868. The First Ten Years of Administration under the Crown. By I. T. PRICHARD, Barrister-at-Law. Two Vols. Demy 8vo. With Map. 21s.

Raphael.—RAPHAEL OF URBINO AND HIS FATHER GIOVANNI SANTI. By J. D. PASSAVANT, formerly Director of the Museum at Frankfort. With Twenty Permanent Photographs. Royal 8vo. Handsomely bound. 31s. 6d.

The SATURDAY REVIEW *says of them,* "*We have seen not a few elegant specimens of Mr. Woodbury's new process, but we have seen none that equal these.*"

Reynolds.—SIR JOSHUA REYNOLDS AS A PORTRAIT PAINTER. AN ESSAY. By J. CHURTON COLLINS, B.A. Balliol College, Oxford. Illustrated by a Series of Portraits of distinguished Beauties of the Court of George III. ; reproduced in Autotype from Proof Impressions of the celebrated Engravings, by VALENTINE GREEN, THOMAS WATSON, F. R. SMITH, E. FISHER, and others. Folio half-morocco. £5 5s.

Rogers (James E. Thorold).—HISTORICAL GLEANINGS : A Series of Sketches. Montague, Walpole, Adam Smith, Cobbett. By Prof. ROGERS. Crown 8vo. 4s. 6d. Second Series. Wiklif, Laud, Wilkes, and Horne Tooke. Crown 8vo. 6s.

Routledge.—CHAPTERS IN THE HISTORY OF POPULAR PROGRESS IN ENGLAND, chiefly in Relation to the Freedom of the Press and Trial by Jury, 1660—1820. With application to later years. By J. ROUTLEDGE. 8vo. 16s.

"*The volume abounds in facts and information, almost always useful and often curious.*"—TIMES.

Rumford.—COUNT RUMFORD'S COMPLETE WORKS, with Memoir, and Notices of his Daughter. By GEORGE ELLIS. Five Vols. 8vo. 4l. 14s. 6d.

Seeley (Professor).—LECTURES AND ESSAYS. By J. R. SEELEY, M.A. Professor of Modern History in the University of Cambridge. 8vo. 10s. 6d.
CONTENTS:—*Roman Imperialism*: 1. *The Great Roman Revolution*; 2. *The Proximate Cause of the Fall of the Roman Empire*; *The Later Empire.* — *Milton's Political Opinions* — *Milton's Poetry* — *Elementary Principles in Art* — *Liberal Education in Universities* — *English in Schools* — *The Church as a Teacher of Morality* — *The Teaching of Politics: an Inaugural Lecture delivered at Cambridge.*

Shelburne.—LIFE OF WILLIAM, EARL OF SHELBURNE, AFTERWARDS FIRST MARQUIS OF LANSDOWNE. With Extracts from his Papers and Correspondence. By Lord EDMOND FITZMAURICE. In Three Vols. 8vo. Vol. I. 1737—1766, 12s.; Vol. II. 1766—1776, 12s.; Vol. III. 1776—1805. 16s.
"*Lord Edmond Fitzmaurice has succeeded in placing before us a wealth of new matter, which, while casting valuable and much-needed light on several obscure passages in the political history of a hundred years ago, has enabled us for the first time to form a clear and consistent idea of his ancestor.*"—SPECTATOR.

Sime.—HISTORY OF GERMANY. By JAMES SIME, M.A. 18mo. 3s. Being Vol. V. of the Historical Course for Schools: Edited by EDWARD A. FREEMAN, D.C.L.
"*This is a remarkably clear and impressive History of Germany.*"—STANDARD.

Squier.—PERU: INCIDENTS OF TRAVEL AND EXPLORATION IN THE LAND OF THE INCAS. By E. G. SQUIER, M.A., F.S.A., late U.S. Commissioner to Peru. With 300 Illustrations. Second Edition. 8vo. 21s.
The TIMES says:—"*No more solid and trustworthy contribution has been made to an accurate knowledge of what are among the most wonderful ruins in the world. The work is really what its title implies. While of the greatest importance as a contribution to Peruvian archæology, it is also a thoroughly entertaining and instructive narrative of travel. Not the least important feature must be considered the numerous well executed illustrations.*"

Strangford.—EGYPTIAN SHRINES AND SYRIAN SEPULCHRES, including a Visit to Palmyra. By EMILY A. BEAUFORT (Viscountess Strangford), Author of "The Eastern Shores of the Adriatic." New Edition. Crown 8vo. 7s. 6d.

Tait.—AN ANALYSIS OF ENGLISH HISTORY, based upon Green's "Short History of the English People." By C. W. A. TAIT, M.A., Assistant Master, Clifton College. Crown 8vo. 3s. 6d.

HISTORY, BIOGRAPHY, TRAVELS, ETC. 27

Tait.—CATHARINE AND CRAUFURD TAIT, WIFE AND SON OF ARCHIBALD CAMPBELL, ARCHBISHOP OF CANTERBURY: a Memoir, Edited, at the request of the Archbishop, by the Rev. W. BENHAM, B.D., Vicar of Margate, and One of the Six Preachers of Canterbury Cathedral. With Two Portraits engraved by JEENS. Crown 8vo. 12s. 6d.

"*The volume can scarcely fail to be read widely and with deep interest. . . . It is difficult to put it down when once taken in hand, still more difficult to get through it without emotion. . . . We commend the volume to those who knew Catharine and Craufurd Tait as one which will bring back to their minds recollections of their characters as true as the recollections of the faces brought back by the two excellent portraits which adorn the book; while to those who knew them not, we commend it as containing the record of two noble Christian lives, which it will be a pleasure to them to contemplate and an advantage to emulate.*"—TIMES.

Thomas.—THE LIFE OF JOHN THOMAS, Surgeon of the "Earl of Oxford" East Indiaman, and First Baptist Missionary to Bengal. By C. B. LEWIS, Baptist Missionary. 8vo. 10s. 6d.

Thompson.—HISTORY OF ENGLAND. By EDITH THOMPSON. Being Vol. II. of the Historical Course for Schools, Edited by EDWARD A. FREEMAN, D.C.L. New Edition, revised and enlarged, with Maps. 18mo. 2s. 6d.

"*Freedom from prejudice, simplicity of style, and accuracy of statement, are the characteristics of this volume. It is a trustworthy text-book, and likely to be generally serviceable in schools.*"—PALL MALL GAZETTE.
"*In its great accuracy and correctness of detail it stands far ahead of the general run of school manuals. Its arrangement, too, is clear, and its style simple and straightforward.*"—SATURDAY REVIEW.

Todhunter.—THE CONFLICT OF STUDIES; AND OTHER ESSAYS ON SUBJECTS CONNECTED WITH EDUCATION. By ISAAC TODHUNTER, M.A., F.R.S., late Fellow and Principal Mathematical Lecturer of St. John's College, Cambridge. 8vo. 10s. 6d.

Trench (Archbishop).—For other Works by the same Author, see THEOLOGICAL and BELLES LETTRES CATALOGUES, and page 30 of this Catalogue.
  GUSTAVUS ADOLPHUS IN GERMANY, and other Lectures on the Thirty Years' War. Second Edition, revised and enlarged. Fcap. 8vo. 4s.
  PLUTARCH, HIS LIFE, HIS LIVES, AND HIS MORALS. Five Lectures. Second Edition, enlarged. Fcap. 8vo. 3s. 6d.
  LECTURES ON MEDIEVAL CHURCH HISTORY. Being the substance of Lectures delivered in Queen's College, London. Second Edition, revised. 8vo. 12s.

Trench (Maria).—THE LIFE OF ST. TERESA. By MARIA TRENCH. With Portrait engraved by JEENS. Crown 8vo, cloth extra. 8s. 6d.

"*A book of rare interest.*"—JOHN BULL.

Trench (Mrs. R.)—REMAINS OF THE LATE MRS. RICHARD TRENCH. Being Selections from her Journals, Letters, and other Papers. Edited by ARCHBISHOP TRENCH. New and Cheaper Issue, with Portrait. 8vo. 6s.

Trollope.—A HISTORY OF THE COMMONWEALTH OF FLORENCE FROM THE EARLIEST INDEPENDENCE OF THE COMMUNE TO THE FALL OF THE REPUBLIC IN 1831. By T. ADOLPHUS TROLLOPE. 4 Vols. 8vo. Half morocco. 21s.

Uppingham by the Sea.—A NARRATIVE OF THE YEAR AT BORTH. By J. H. S. Crown 8vo. 3s. 6d.

Victor Emmanuel II., First King of Italy.—HIS LIFE. By G. S. GODKIN. 2 vols., crown 8vo. 16s.

"*An extremely clear and interesting history of one of the most important changes of later times.*"—EXAMINER.

Wallace.—THE MALAY ARCHIPELAGO: the Land of the Orang Utan and the Bird of Paradise. By ALFRED RUSSEL WALLACE. A Narrative of Travel with Studies of Man and Nature. With Maps and numerous Illustrations. Sixth Edition. Crown 8vo. 7s. 6d.

"*The result is a vivid picture of tropical life, which may be read with unflagging interest, and a sufficient account of his scientific conclusions to stimulate our appetite without wearying us by detail. In short, we may safely say that we have never read a more agreeable book of its kind.*"—SATURDAY REVIEW.

Ward.—A HISTORY OF ENGLISH DRAMATIC LITERATURE TO THE DEATH OF QUEEN ANNE. By A. W. WARD, M.A., Professor of History and English Literature in Owens College, Manchester. Two Vols. 8vo. 32s.

"*As full of interest as of information. To students of dramatic literature invaluable, and may be equally recommended to readers for mere pastime.*"—PALL MALL GAZETTE.

Ward (J.)—EXPERIENCES OF A DIPLOMATIST. Being recollections of Germany founded on Diaries kept during the years 1840—1870. By JOHN WARD, C.B., late H.M. Minister-Resident to the Hanse Towns. 8vo. 10s. 6d.

Waterton (C.)—WANDERINGS IN SOUTH AMERICA, THE NORTH-WEST OF THE UNITED STATES, AND THE ANTILLES IN 1812, 1816, 1820, and 1824. With Original Instructions for the perfect Preservation of Birds, etc., for Cabinets of Natural History. By CHARLES WATERTON. New Edition, edited with Biographical Introduction and Explanatory Index by the Rev. J. G. WOOD, M.A. With 100 Illustrations. Cheaper Edition. Crown 8vo. 6s.

Wedgwood.—JOHN WESLEY AND THE EVANGELICAL REACTION of the Eighteenth Century. By JULIA WEDGWOOD. Crown 8vo. 8s. 6d.

Whewell.—WILLIAM WHEWELL, D.D., late Master of Trinity College, Cambridge. An Account of his Writings, with Selections from his Literary and Scientific Correspondence. By I. TODHUNTER, M.A., F.R.S. Two Vols. 8vo. 25s.

White.—THE NATURAL HISTORY AND ANTIQUITIES OF SELBORNE. By GILBERT WHITE. Edited, with Memoir and Notes, by FRANK BUCKLAND, A Chapter on Antiquities by LORD SELBORNE, Map, &c., and numerous Illustrations by P. H. DELAMOTTE. Royal 8vo. Cloth, extra gilt. Cheaper Issue. 21s.

Also a Large Paper Edition, containing, in addition to the above, upwards of Thirty Woodburytype Illustrations from Drawings by Prof. DELAMOTTE. Two Vols. 4to. Half morocco, elegant. 4l. 4s.

"*Mr. Delamotte's charming illustrations are a worthy decoration of so dainty a book. They bring Selborne before us, and really help us to understand why White's love for his native place never grew cold.*"—TIMES.

Wilson.—A MEMOIR OF GEORGE WILSON, M.D., F.R.S.E., Regius Professor of Technology in the University of Edinburgh. By his SISTER. New Edition. Crown 8vo. 6s.

Wilson (Daniel, LL.D.)—Works by DANIEL WILSON, LL.D., Professor of History and English Literature in University College, Toronto:—

PREHISTORIC ANNALS OF SCOTLAND. New Edition, with numerous Illustrations. Two Vols. demy 8vo. 36s.

"*One of the most interesting, learned, and elegant works we have seen for a long time.*"—WESTMINSTER REVIEW.

PREHISTORIC MAN: Researches into the Origin of Civilization in the Old and New World. New Edition, revised and enlarged throughout, with numerous Illustrations and two Coloured Plates. Two Vols. 8vo. 36s.

Wilson.—*continued.*

"A valuable work pleasantly written and well worthy of attention both by students and general readers."—ACADEMY.

> CHATTERTON: A Biographical Study. By DANIEL WILSON, LL.D., Professor of History and English Literature in University College, Toronto. Crown 8vo. 6s. 6d.

Yonge (Charlotte M.)—Works by CHARLOTTE M. YONGE, Author of "The Heir of Redclyffe," &c., &c. :—

> A PARALLEL HISTORY OF FRANCE AND ENGLAND: consisting of Outlines and Dates. Oblong 4to. 3s. 6d.

> CAMEOS FROM ENGLISH HISTORY. From Rollo to Edward II. Extra fcap. 8vo. Third Edition. 5s.

> SECOND SERIES, THE WARS IN FRANCE. Extra fcap. 8vo. Third Edition. 5s.

> THIRD SERIES, THE WARS OF THE ROSES. Extra fcap. 8vo. 5s.

"Instead of dry details," says the NONCONFORMIST, *"we have living pictures, faithful, vivid, and striking."*

> FOURTH SERIES. Reformation Times. Extra fcap. 8vo. 5s.

> HISTORY OF FRANCE. Maps. 18mo. 3s. 6d.
> [*Historical Course for Schools.*

POLITICS, POLITICAL AND SOCIAL ECONOMY, LAW, AND KINDRED SUBJECTS.

Anglo-Saxon Law.—ESSAYS IN. Contents: Law Courts—Land and Family Laws and Legal Procedure generally. With Select cases. Medium 8vo. 18s.

Arnold.—THE ROMAN SYSTEM OF PROVINCIAL ADMINISTRATION TO THE ACCESSION OF CONSTANTINE THE GREAT. Being the Arnold Prize Essay for 1879. By W. T. Arnold, B.A. Crown 8vo. 6s.

Ball.—THE STUDENT'S GUIDE TO THE BAR. By WALTER W. BALL, M.A., of the Inner Temple, Barrister-at-Law. Crown 8vo. 2s. 6d.
"*The student will here find a clear statement of the several steps by which the degree of barrister is obtained, and also useful advice about the advantages of a prolonged course of 'reading in Chambers.'*"—ACADEMY.

Bernard.—FOUR LECTURES ON SUBJECTS CONNECTED WITH DIPLOMACY. By MONTAGUE BERNARD, M.A., Chichele Professor of International Law and Diplomacy, Oxford. 8vo. 9s.
"*Singularly interesting lectures, so able, clear, and attractive.*"—SPECTATOR.

Bright (John, M.P.)—Works by the Right Hon. JOHN BRIGHT, M.P.

SPEECHES ON QUESTIONS OF PUBLIC POLICY. Edited by Professor THOROLD ROGERS. Author's Popular Edition. Globe 8vo. 3s. 6d.
"*Mr. Bright's speeches will always deserve to be studied, as an apprenticeship to popular and parliamentary oratory; they will form materials for the history of our time, and many brilliant passages, perhaps some entire speeches, will really become a part of the living literature of England.*"—DAILY NEWS.

LIBRARY EDITION. Two Vols. 8vo. With Portrait. 25s.

PUBLIC ADDRESSES. Edited by J. THOROLD ROGERS. 8vo. 14s.

Bucknill.—HABITUAL DRUNKENNESS AND INSANE DRUNKARDS. By J. C. BUCKNILL, M.D., F.R.S., late Lord Chancellor's Visitor of Lunatics. Crown 8vo. 2s. 6d.

Cairnes.—Works by J. E. CAIRNES, M.A., Emeritus Professor of Political Economy in University College, London.
ESSAYS IN POLITICAL ECONOMY, THEORETICAL and APPLIED. By J. E. CAIRNES, M.A., Professor of Political Economy in University College, London. 8vo. 10s. 6d.
POLITICAL ESSAYS. 8vo. 10s. 6d.
SOME LEADING PRINCIPLES OF POLITICAL ECONOMY NEWLY EXPOUNDED. 8vo. 14s.
CONTENTS:—*Part I. Value. Part II. Labour and Capital. Part III. International Trade.*
"*A work which is perhaps the most valuable contribution to the science made since the publication, a quarter of a century since, of Mr. Mill's 'Principles of Political Economy.'*"—DAILY NEWS.
THE CHARACTER AND LOGICAL METHOD OF POLITICAL ECONOMY. New Edition, enlarged. 8vo. 7s. 6d.
"*These lectures are admirably fitted to correct the slipshod generalizations which pass current as the science of Political Economy.*"—TIMES.

Cobden (Richard).—SPEECHES ON QUESTIONS OF PUBLIC POLICY. By RICHARD COBDEN. Edited by the Right Hon. John Bright, M.P., and J. E. Thorold Rogers. Popular Edition. 8vo. 3s. 6d.

Fawcett.—Works by HENRY FAWCETT, M.A., M.P., Fellow of Trinity Hall, and Professor of Political Economy in the University of Cambridge:—
THE ECONOMIC POSITION OF THE BRITISH LABOURER. Extra fcap. 8vo. 5s.
MANUAL OF POLITICAL ECONOMY. Fifth Edition, with New Chapters on the Depreciation of Silver, etc. Crown 8vo. 12s.
The DAILY NEWS *says:* "*It forms one of the best introductions to the principles of the science, and to its practical applications in the problems of modern, and especially of English, government and society.*"
PAUPERISM: ITS CAUSES AND REMEDIES. Crown 8vo. 5s. 6d.
The ATHENÆUM *calls the work* "*a repertory of interesting and well digested information.*"
SPEECHES ON SOME CURRENT POLITICAL QUESTIONS. 8vo. 10s. 6d.
"*They will help to educate, not perhaps, parties, but the educators of parties.*"—DAILY NEWS.

Fawcett.—*continued.*
FREE TRADE AND PROTECTION: an Inquiry into the Causes which have retarded the general adoption of Free Trade since its introduction into England. Third Edition. 8vo. 7s. 6d.
"*No greater service can be rendered to the cause of Free Trade than a clear explanation of the principles on which Free Trade rests. Professor Fawcett has done this in the volume before us with all his habitual clearness of thought and expression.*"—ECONOMIST.

ESSAYS ON POLITICAL AND SOCIAL SUBJECTS. By PROFESSOR FAWCETT, M.P., and MILLICENT GARRETT FAWCETT. 8vo. 10s. 6d.
"*They will all repay the perusal of the thinking reader.*"—DAILY NEWS.

Fawcett (Mrs.)—Works by MILLICENT GARRETT FAWCETT.
POLITICAL ECONOMY FOR BEGINNERS. WITH QUESTIONS. New Edition. 18mo. 2s. 6d.
The DAILY NEWS *calls it "clear, compact, and comprehensive;" and the* SPECTATOR *says, "Mrs. Fawcett's treatise is perfectly suited to its purpose."*

TALES IN POLITICAL ECONOMY. Crown 8vo. 3s.
"*The idea is a good one, and it is quite wonderful what a mass of economic teaching the author manages to compress into a small space... The true doctrines of International Trade, Currency, and the ratio between Production and Population, are set before us and illustrated in a masterly manner.*"—ATHENÆUM.

Freeman (E. A.), M.A., D.C.L.—COMPARATIVE POLITICS. Lectures at the Royal Institution, to which is added "The Unity of History," being the Rede Lecture delivered at Cambridge in 1872. 8vo. 14s.
"*We find in Mr. Freeman's new volume the same sound, careful, comprehensive qualities which have long ago raised him to so high a place amongst historical writers. For historical discipline, then, as well as historical information, Mr. Freeman's book is full of value.*"—PALL MALL GAZETTE.

Goschen.—REPORTS AND SPEECHES ON LOCAL TAXATION. By GEORGE J. GOSCHEN, M.P. Royal 8vo. 5s.
"*The volume contains a vast mass of information of the highest value.*"—ATHENÆUM.

Guide to the Unprotected, in Every Day Matters Relating to Property and Income. By a BANKER'S DAUGHTER. Fourth Edition, Revised. Extra fcap. 8vo. 3s. 6d.

"*Many an unprotected female will bless the head which planned and the hand which compiled this admirable little manual. . . . This book was very much wanted, and it could not have been better done.*"— MORNING STAR.

Hamilton.—MONEY AND VALUE: an Inquiry into the Means and Ends of Economic Production, with an Appendix on the Depreciation of Silver and Indian Currency. By ROWLAND HAMILTON. 8vo. 12s.

"*The subject is here dealt with in a luminous style, and by presenting it from a new point of view in connection with the nature and functions of money, a genuine service has been rendered to commercial science.*"— BRITISH QUARTERLY REVIEW.

Harwood.—DISESTABLISHMENT: a Defence of the Principle of a National Church. By GEORGE HARWOOD, M.A. 8vo. 12s.

Hill.—OUR COMMON LAND; and other Short Essays. By OCTAVIA HILL. Extra fcap. 8vo. 3s. 6d.
CONTENTS:—*Our Common Land. District Visiting. A More Excellent Way of Charity. A Word on Good Citizenship. Open Spaces. Effectual Charity. The Future of our Commons.*

Historicus.—LETTERS ON SOME QUESTIONS OF INTERNATIONAL LAW. Reprinted from the *Times*, with considerable Additions. 8vo. 7s. 6d. Also, ADDITIONAL LETTERS. 8vo. 2s. 6d.

Holland.—THE TREATY RELATIONS OF RUSSIA AND TURKEY FROM 1774 TO 1853. A Lecture delivered at Oxford, April 1877. By T. E. HOLLAND, D.C.L., Professor of International Law and Diplomacy, Oxford. Crown 8vo. 2s.

Hughes (Thos.)—THE OLD CHURCH: WHAT SHALL WE DO WITH IT? By THOMAS HUGHES, Q.C. Crown 8vo. 6s.

Jevons.—Works by W. STANLEY JEVONS, M.A., Professor of Political Economy in University College, London. (For other Works by the same Author, see EDUCATIONAL and PHILOSOPHICAL CATALOGUES.)

THE THEORY OF POLITICAL ECONOMY. Second Edition, revised, with new Preface and Appendices. 8vo. 10s. 6d.

"*Professor Jevons has done invaluable service by courageously claiming political economy to be strictly a branch of Applied Mathematics.*" —WESTMINSTER REVIEW.

PRIMER OF POLITICAL ECONOMY. 18mo. 1s.

WORKS IN POLITICS, ETC.

Laveleye. — PRIMITIVE PROPERTY. By EMILE DE LAVELEYE. Translated by G. R. L. MARRIOTT, LL.B., with an Introduction by T. E. CLIFFE LESLIE, LL.B. 8vo. 12s.

"*It is almost impossible to over-estimate the value of the well-digested knowledge which it contains; it is one of the most learned books that have been contributed to the historical department of the literature of economic science.*"—ATHENÆUM.

Leading Cases done into English. By an APPRENTICE OF LINCOLN'S INN. Third Edition. Crown 8vo. 2s. 6d.

"*Here is a rare treat for the lovers of quaint conceits, who in reading this charming little book will find enjoyment in the varied metre and graphic language in which the several tales are told, no less than in the accurate and pithy rendering of some of our most familiar 'Leading Cases.'*"—SATURDAY REVIEW.

Lubbock.—ADDRESSES, POLITICAL AND EDUCATIONAL. By Sir JOHN LUBBOCK, Bart., M.P., &c., &c. 8vo, pp. 209. 8s. 6d.

The ten speeches given are (1) on the Imperial Policy of Great Britain, (2) on the Bank Act of 1844, (3) on the Present System of Public School Education, 1876, (4) on the Present System of Elementary Education. (5) on the Income Tax, (6) on the National Debt, (7) on the Declaration of Paris, (8) on Marine Insurances, (9) on the Preservation of Ancient Monuments, and (10) on Egypt.

Macdonell.—THE LAND QUESTION, WITH SPECIAL REFERENCE TO ENGLAND AND SCOTLAND. By JOHN MACDONELL, Barrister-at-Law. 8vo. 10s. 6d.

Marshall.—THE ECONOMICS OF INDUSTRY. By A. MARSHALL, M.A., Principal of University College, Bristol, and MARY PALEY MARSHALL, late Lecturer at Newnham Hall, Cambridge. Extra fcap. 8vo. 2s. 6d.

Martin.—THE STATESMAN'S YEAR-BOOK: A Statistical and Historical Annual of the States of the Civilized World, for the year 1880. By FREDERICK MARTIN. Seventeenth Annual Publication. Revised after Official Returns. Crown 8vo. 10s. 6d.

The Statesman's Year-Book is the only work in the English language which furnishes a clear and concise account of the actual condition of all the States of Europe, the civilized countries of America, Asia, and Africa, and the British Colonies and Dependencies in all parts of the world. The new issue of the work has been revised and corrected, on the basis of official reports received direct from the heads of the leading Governments of the world, in reply to letters sent to them by the Editor. Through the valuable assistance thus given, it has been possible to collect an amount of information, political, statistical, and commercial, of the latest date, and of unimpeachable trustworthiness, such as no publication of the same kind has ever been able to furnish. "As indispensable as Bradshaw."—TIMES.

Monahan.—THE METHOD OF LAW: an Essay on the Statement and Arrangement of the Legal Standard of Conduct. By J. H. MONAHAN, Q.C. Crown 8vo. 6s.
"*Will be found valuable by careful law students who have felt the importance of gaining clear ideas regarding the relations between the parts of the complex organism they have to study.*"—BRITISH QUARTERLY REVIEW.

Paterson.—THE LIBERTY OF THE SUBJECT AND THE LAWS OF ENGLAND RELATING TO THE SECURITY OF THE PERSON. Commentaries on. By JAMES PATERSON, M.A., Barrister at Law, sometime Commissioner for English and Irish Fisheries, etc. Cheaper issue. Two Vols. Crown 8vo. 21s.
"*Two or three hours' dipping into these volumes, not to say reading them through, will give legislators and stump orators a knowledge of the liberty of a citizen of their country, in its principles, its fulness, and its modification, such as they probably in nine cases out of ten never had before.*"—SCOTSMAN.

Phillimore.—PRIVATE LAW AMONG THE ROMANS, from the Pandects. By JOHN GEORGE PHILLIMORE, Q.C. 8vo. 16s.

Rogers.—COBDEN AND POLITICAL OPINION. By J. E. THOROLD ROGERS. 8vo. 10s. 6d.
"*Will be found most useful by politicians of every school, as it forms a sort of handbook to Cobden's teaching.*"—ATHENÆUM.

Stephen (C. E.)—THE SERVICE OF THE POOR; Being an Inquiry into the Reasons for and against the Establishment of Religious Sisterhoods for Charitable Purposes. By CAROLINE EMILIA STEPHEN. Crown 8vo. 6s. 6d.
"*The ablest advocate of a better line of work in this direction that we have ever seen.*"—EXAMINER.

Stephen.—Works by Sir JAMES F. STEPHEN, K.C.S.I., Q.C.
A DIGEST OF THE LAW OF EVIDENCE. Third Edition with New Preface. Crown 8vo. 6s.
A DIGEST OF THE CRIMINAL LAW. (Crimes and Punishments.) 8vo. 16s.
"*We feel sure that any person of ordinary intelligence who had never looked into a law-book in his life might, by a few days' careful study of*

WORKS IN POLITICS, ETC.

Stephen.—*continued.*

this volume, obtain a more accurate understanding of the criminal law, a more perfect conception of its different bearings, a more thorough and intelligent insight into its snares and pitfalls, than an ordinary practitioner can boast of after years of study of the ordinary textbooks and practical experience of the Courts unassisted by any competent guide."—SATURDAY REVIEW.

    A GENERAL VIEW OF THE CRIMINAL LAW OF ENGLAND. Two Vols. Crown 8vo. [*New edition in the press.*

Stubbs.—VILLAGE POLITICS. Addresses and Sermons on the Labour Question. By C. W. STUBBS, M.A., Vicar of Granborough, Bucks. Extra fcap. 8vo. 3s. 6d.

Thornton.—Works by W. T. THORNTON, C.B., Secretary for Public Works in the India Office :—

    ON LABOUR: Its Wrongful Claims and Rightful Dues; Its Actual Present and Possible Future. Second Edition, revised, 8vo. 14s.

    A PLEA FOR PEASANT PROPRIETORS : With the Outlines of a Plan for their Establishment in Ireland. New Edition, revised. Crown 8vo. 7s. 6d.

    INDIAN PUBLIC WORKS AND COGNATE INDIAN TOPICS. With Map of Indian Railways. Crown 8vo. 8s. 6d.

Walker.—Works by F. A. WALKER, M.A., Ph.D., Professor of Political Economy and History, Yale College :—

    THE WAGES QUESTION. A Treatise on Wages and the Wages Class. 8vo. 14s.

    MONEY. 8vo. 16s.

" *It is painstaking, laborious, and states the question in a clear and very intelligible form. . . . The volume possesses a great value as a sort of encyclopædia of knowledge on the subject.*"—ECONOMIST.

    MONEY IN ITS RELATIONS TO TRADE AND INDUSTRY. Crown 8vo. [*Shortly.*

Work about the Five Dials. With an Introductory Note by THOMAS CARLYLE. Crown 8vo. 6s.

"*A book which abounds with wise and practical suggestions.*"—PALL MALL GAZETTE.

WORKS CONNECTED WITH THE SCIENCE OR THE HISTORY OF LANGUAGE.

Abbott.—A SHAKESPERIAN GRAMMAR: An Attempt to illustrate some of the Differences between Elizabethan and Modern English. By the Rev. E. A. ABBOTT, D.D., Head Master of the City of London School. New and Enlarged Edition. Extra fcap. 8vo. 6s.

"*Valuable not only as an aid to the critical study of Shakespeare, but as tending to familiarize the reader with Elizabethan English in general.*"—ATHENÆUM.

Breymann.—A FRENCH GRAMMAR BASED ON PHILOLOGICAL PRINCIPLES. By HERMANN BREYMANN, Ph.D., Professor of Philology in the University of Munich late Lecturer on French Language and Literature at Owens College, Manchester. Extra fcap. 8vo. 4s. 6d.

Ellis.—PRACTICAL HINTS ON THE QUANTITATIVE PRONUNCIATION OF LATIN, FOR THE USE OF CLASSICAL TEACHERS AND LINGUISTS. By A. J. ELLIS, B.A., F.R.S., &c. Extra fcap. 8vo. 4s. 6d.

Fleay.—A SHAKESPEARE MANUAL. By the Rev. F. G. FLEAY, M.A., Head Master of Skipton Grammar School. Extra fcap. 8vo. 4s. 6d.

Goodwin.—Works by W. W. GOODWIN, Professor of Greek Literature in Harvard University.

SYNTAX OF THE GREEK MOODS AND TENSES. New Edition. Crown 8vo. 6s. 6d.

AN ELEMENTARY GREEK GRAMMAR. Crown 8vo. 6s.

"*It is the best Greek Grammar of its size in the English language.*"—ATHENÆUM.

Hadley.—ESSAYS PHILOLOGICAL AND CRITICAL. Selected from the Papers of JAMES HADLEY, LL.D., Professor of Greek in Yale College, &c. 8vo. 16s.

Hales.—LONGER ENGLISH POEMS. With Notes, Philological and Explanatory, and an Introduction on the Teaching of English. Chiefly for use in Schools. Edited by J. W. HALES, M.A., Professor of English Literature at King's College, London, &c. &c. Fifth Edition. Extra fcap. 8vo. 4s. 6d.

Helfenstein (James).—A COMPARATIVE GRAMMAR OF THE TEUTONIC LANGUAGES: Being at the same time a Historical Grammar of the English Language, and comprising Gothic, Anglo-Saxon, Early English, Modern English, Icelandic (Old Norse), Danish, Swedish, Old High German, Middle High German, Modern German, Old Saxon, Old Frisian, and Dutch. By JAMES HELFENSTEIN, Ph.D. 8vo. 18s.

Masson (Gustave).—A COMPENDIOUS DICTIONARY OF THE FRENCH LANGUAGE (French-English and English-French). Followed by a List of the Principal Diverging Derivations, and preceded by Chronological and Historical Tables. By GUSTAVE MASSON, Assistant-Master and Librarian, Harrow School. Fourth Edition. Crown 8vo. Half-bound. 6s.

"*A book which any student, whatever may be the degree of his advancement in the language, would do well to have on the table close at hand while he is reading.*"—SATURDAY REVIEW.

Mayor.—A BIBLIOGRAPHICAL CLUE TO LATIN LITERATURE. Edited after Dr. E. HUBNER. With large Additions by JOHN E. B. MAYOR, M.A., Professor of Latin in the University of Cambridge. Crown 8vo. 6s. 6d.

"*An extremely useful volume that should be in the hands of all scholars.*"—ATHENÆUM.

Morris.—Works by the Rev. RICHARD MORRIS, LL.D., Member of the Council of the Philol. Soc., Lecturer on English Language and Literature in King's College School, Editor of "Specimens of Early English," etc., etc.:—

HISTORICAL OUTLINES OF ENGLISH ACCIDENCE, comprising Chapters on the History and Development of the Language, and on Word-formation. Sixth Edition. Fcap. 8vo. 6s.

ELEMENTARY LESSONS IN HISTORICAL ENGLISH GRAMMAR, containing Accidence and Word-formation. Third Edition. 18mo. 2s. 6d.

Oliphant.—THE OLD AND MIDDLE ENGLISH. By T. L. KINGTON OLIPHANT, M.A., of Balliol College, Oxford. A New Edition, revised and greatly enlarged, of "The Sources of Standard English." Extra fcap. 8vo. 9s.

"*Mr. Oliphant's book is to our mind, one of the ablest and most scholarly contributions to our standard English we have seen for many years.*"—SCHOOL BOARD CHRONICLE. "*The book comes nearer to a history of the English language than anything we have seen since such a history could be written, without confusion and contradictions.*"—SATURDAY REVIEW.

Peile (John, M.A.)—AN INTRODUCTION TO GREEK AND LATIN ETYMOLOGY. By JOHN PEILE, M.A., Fellow and Tutor of Christ's College, Cambridge. Third and revised Edition. Crown 8vo. 10s. 6d.

"*The book may be accepted as a very valuable contribution to the science of language.*"—SATURDAY REVIEW.

Philology.—THE JOURNAL OF SACRED AND CLASSICAL PHILOLOGY. Four Vols. 8vo. 12s. 6d. each.

THE JOURNAL OF PHILOLOGY. New Series. Edited by JOHN E. B. MAYOR, M.A., and W. ALDIS WRIGHT, M.A. 4s. 6d. (Half-yearly.)

Roby (H. J.)—A GRAMMAR OF THE LATIN LANGUAGE, FROM PLAUTUS TO SUETONIUS. By HENRY JOHN ROBY, M.A., late Fellow of St. John's College, Cambridge. In Two Parts. Second Edition. Part I. containing:—Book I. Sounds. Book II. Inflexions. Book III. Word Formation. Appendices. Crown 8vo. 8s. 6d. Part II.—Syntax, Prepositions, &c. Crown 8vo. 10s. 6d.

"*The book is marked by the clear and practical insight of a master in his art. It is a book which would do honour to any country.*"—ATHENÆUM. "*Brings before the student in a methodical form the best results of modern philology bearing on the Latin language.*"—SCOTSMAN.

Schmidt.—THE RYTHMIC AND METRIC OF THE CLASSICAL LANGUAGES. To which are added, the Lyric Parts of the "Medea" of Euripides and the "Antigone" of Sophocles; with Rhythmical Scheme and Commentary. By Dr. J. H. SCHMIDT. Translated from the German by J. W. WHITE, D.D. 8vo. 10s. 6d.

Taylor.—Works by the Rev. ISAAC TAYLOR, M.A.:—

ETRUSCAN RESEARCHES. With Woodcuts. 8vo. 14s.

The TIMES says:—"*The learning and industry displayed in this volume deserve the most cordial recognition. The ultimate verdict of science we shall not attempt to anticipate; but we can safely say this, that it is a learned book which the unlearned can enjoy, and that in the descriptions of the tomb-builders, as well as in the marvellous coincidences and unexpected analogies brought together by the author, readers of every grade may take delight as well as philosophers and scholars.*"

WORDS AND PLACES; or, Etymological Illustrations of History, Ethnology, and Geography. By the Rev. ISAAC TAYLOR. Third Edition, revised and compressed. With Maps. Globe 8vo. 6s.

GREEKS AND GOTHS: a Study on the Runes. 8vo. 9s.

WORKS ON LANGUAGE. 41

Trench.—Works by R. CHENEVIX TRENCH, D.D., Archbishop of Dublin. (For other Works by the same Author, *see* THEOLOGICAL CATALOGUE.)

SYNONYMS OF THE NEW TESTAMENT. Eighth Edition, enlarged. 8vo, cloth. 12s.

"*He is,*" the ATHENÆUM *says, "a guide in this department of knowledge to whom his readers may entrust themselves with confidence.*"

ON THE STUDY OF WORDS. Lectures Addressed (originally) to the Pupils at the Diocesan Training School, Winchester. Seventeenth Edition, enlarged. Fcap. 8vo. 5s.

ENGLISH PAST AND PRESENT. Tenth Edition, revised and improved. Fcap. 8vo. 5s.

A SELECT GLOSSARY OF ENGLISH WORDS USED FORMERLY IN SENSES DIFFERENT FROM THEIR PRESENT. Fifth Edition, enlarged. Fcap. 8vo. 5s.

Vincent and Dickson.—A HANDBOOK TO MODERN GREEK. By EDGAR VINCENT and T. G. DICKSON. Extra fcap. 8vo. 5s.

Whitney.—A COMPENDIOUS GERMAN GRAMMAR. By W. D. WHITNEY, Professor of Sanskrit and Instructor in Modern Languages in Yale College. Crown 8vo. 6s.

"*After careful examination we are inclined to pronounce it the best grammar of modern language we have ever seen.*"—SCOTSMAN.

Whitney and Edgren.—A COMPENDIOUS GERMAN AND ENGLISH DICTIONARY, with Notation of Correspondences and Brief Etymologies. By Professor W. D. WHITNEY, assisted by A. H. EDGREN. Crown 8vo. 7s. 6d.

The GERMAN-ENGLISH Part may be had separately. Price 5s.

Yonge.—HISTORY OF CHRISTIAN NAMES. By CHARLOTTE M. YONGE, Author of "The Heir of Redclyffe." Cheaper Edition. Two Vols. Crown 8vo. 12s.

Now publishing, in crown 8vo, price 2s. 6d. each.

ENGLISH MEN OF LETTERS.

Edited by JOHN MORLEY.

A Series of Short Books to tell people what is best worth knowing to the Life, Character, and Works of some of the great English Writers.

ENGLISH MEN OF LETTERS.—JOHNSON. By LESLIE STEPHEN.

"The new series opens well with Mr. Leslie Stephen's sketch of Dr. Johnson. It could hardly have been done better, and it will convey to the readers for whom it is intended a juster estimate of Johnson than either of the two essays of Lord Macaulay."—*Pall Mall Gazette*

ENGLISH MEN OF LETTERS.—SCOTT. By R. H. HUTTON.

"The tone of the volume is excellect throughout."—*Athenæum.*

"We could not wish for a more suggestive introduction to Scott and his poems and novels."—*Examiner.*

ENGLISH MEN OF LETTERS.—GIBBON. By J. C. MORISON.

"As a clear, thoughtful, and attractive record of the life and works of the greatest among the world's historians, it deserves the highest praise."—*Examiner.*

ENGLISH MEN OF LETTERS.—SHELLEY. By J. A. SYMONDS.

"The lovers of this great poet are to be congratulated on having at their command so fresh, clear, and intelligent a presentment of the subject, written by a man of adequate and wide culture."—*Athenæum.*

ENGLISH MEN OF LETTERS.—HUME. By Professor HUXLEY.

"It may fairly be said that no one now living could have expounded Hume with more sympathy or with equal perspicuity."—*Athenæum.*

ENGLISH MEN OF LETTERS. — GOLDSMITH. By WILLIAM BLACK.

"Mr. Black brings a fine sympathy and taste to bear in his criticism of Goldsmith's writings, as well as in his sketch of the incidents of his life."—*Athenæum.*

ENGLISH MEN OF LETTERS.—DEFOE. By W. MINTO.

"Mr. Minto's book is careful and accurate in all that is stated, and faithful in all that it suggests. It will repay reading more than once."—*Athenæum.*

ENGLISH MEN OF LETTERS—*Continued.*

ENGLISH MEN OF LETTERS.—BURNS. By Principal SHAIRP, Professor of Poetry in the University of Oxford.

"It is impossible to desire fairer criticism than Principal Shairp's on Burns's poetry. . . . . None of the series has given a truer estimate either of character or of genius than this little volume. . . . and all who read it will be thoroughly grateful to the author for this monument to the genius of Scotland's greatest poet."—*Spectator.*

ENGLISH MEN OF LETTERS.—SPENSER. By the Very Rev. the DEAN OF ST. PAUL'S.

"Dr. Church is master of his subject, and writes always with good taste."—*Academy.*

ENGLISH MEN OF LETTERS.—THACKERAY. By ANTHONY TROLLOPE.

"Mr. Trollope's sketch is exceedingly adapted to fulfil the purpose of the series in which it appears."—*Athenæum.*

ENGLISH MEN OF LETTERS.—BURKE. By JOHN MORLEY.

"Perhaps the best criticism yet published on the life and character of Burke is contained in Mr. Morley's compendious biography. His style is vigorous and polished, and both his political and personal judgment and his literary criticisms are just, generous, subtle, and in a high degree interesting."—*Saturday Review.*

Just ready.

MILTON. By MARK PATTISON.

In preparation.

HAWTHORNE. By HENRY JAMES.

SOUTHEY. By Professor DOWDEN.

CHAUCER. By Professor WARD.

COWPER. By GOLDWIN SMITH.

BUNYAN. By J. A. FROUDE.

WORDSWORTH. By F. W. H. MYERS.

Others in preparation.

MACMILLAN AND CO., LONDON.

LONDON:
R. CLAY, SONS, AND TAYLOR, PRINTERS,
BREAD STREET HILL.

www.ingramcontent.com/pod-product-compliance
Lightning Source LLC
Chambersburg PA
CBHW020250170426
43202CB00008B/302